TRANSFORMING TRAUMA

TRANSFORMING TRAUMA

HOW YOU CAN TURN YOUR PAIN INTO POWER

MELISSA L. CARR

NEW DEGREE PRESS
COPYRIGHT © 2021 MELISSA L. CARR
All rights reserved.

TRANSFORMING TRAUMA
How You Can Turn Your Pain into Power

ISBN   978-1-63730-805-9 *Paperback*
            978-1-63730-864-6 *Kindle Ebook*
            978-1-63730-983-4 *Ebook*

Unless otherwise indicated, Bible verses are taken from the Holy Bible, Scripture taken from the King James Version®. Courtesy of INT Bible Copyright © 2012. Used by Permission. All rights reserved.

Other Scripture references used throughout are taken from the following Bible translations:

New King James Version (NKJV)
New King James Version®. Copyright © 1982 by Thomas Nelson. Used by permission. All rights reserved.

New International Version (NIV)
Holy Bible, New International Version®, NIV® Copyright © 1973, 1978, 1984, 2011 by Biblica, Inc.® Used by permission. All rights reserved worldwide.

English Standard Version (ESV)
The Holy Bible, English Standard Version. ESV® Text Edition: 2016. Copyright © 2001 by Crossway Bibles, a publishing ministry of Good News Publishers.

This book is dedicated to all of the caterpillars preparing to transform into beautiful butterflies.

This book is dedicated to my mother, Bonnie, who happens to be my number one cheerleader. Thank you for rocking out with me throughout my entire life, hanging in there throughout the times of adversity, and literally telling me to put my hands up for this rollercoaster of a journey. We have arrived.

CONTENTS

PROLOGUE 11
INTRODUCTION. 21

CHAPTER 1.   MY DREAM JOB 33
CHAPTER 2.   MY PLAN VS. GOD'S PLAN 49
CHAPTER 3.   BETRAYAL 67
CHAPTER 4.   THE PROCESS OF GRIEF 85
CHAPTER 5.   BROKEN BUT NOT FORGOTTEN 95
CHAPTER 6.   THE PURPOSE OF ADVERSITY 109
CHAPTER 7.   ABANDONMENT. 123
CHAPTER 8.   THE POWER OF A POSITIVE THOUGHT 137
CHAPTER 9.   HAPPINESS IS AN INSIDE JOB 149
CHAPTER 10. UNPLUG, RECHARGE, AND RESET 159
CHAPTER 11. CONCLUSION: DEALING WITH TRAUMA 171

ACKNOWLEDGMENTS. 177
APPENDIX. 181

In my experience, happiness isn't money. Happiness is when you're able to wake up each day and look yourself straight in the eyes without regret while knowing life hasn't been and still isn't perfect! You then have control of your happiness.

MELISSA CARR

PROLOGUE

"You restored me to health and let me live. Surely it was for my benefit I suffered such anguish. In your love, you kept me from the pit of destruction; you have put all my sins behind your back."

ISAIAH 38:16–17, NIV

I am sharing with the world in an effort to create hope for anyone who may be dealing with challenging times resulting from a traumatic experience or related to illness.

You, too, can grow through your pain and move forward in life.

2020 was the year of the pandemic, everyone went through some form of trauma, whether it be directly or by way of a family member or friend. Don't be so hard on yourself; give yourself a little grace. God placed this idea on my heart some time ago, but, you know, we tend to procrastinate. We try to find the perfect time. But, my friends, I was ordered to do this in His timing which is the only perfect time. God said,

"Now is the time." So, I thought, *why not be obedient?* He has been more than good to me on this journey.

I am going to share with you part of my story. God said, "Get this part out to my people now."

My prayer is you find this book helpful. That little voice that gives you that extra push to keep you going and that constant reminder to **never give up**. The little voice I am referring to has a tendency of pushing me out of my own way. We have conversations—yes, those pep talks that give me that extra boost to keep moving forward. It's like I walk around with my personal cheerleader, blocking out the negativity of the world. I know it seems the entire world has been in survival mode for too long, so it's time for you to start your healing process today! This is my testimony of how I turned my pain into power after a traumatic experience, and I will be demonstrating how you can too!

To some, this may be coffee or tea to sip on. My prayer is you will embrace the techniques in this book and walk away a brand-new person, or at least feeling refreshed from another person's perspective. Most importantly, it's my mission and God's plan over my life to inspire, encourage, and empower. Remember, I only share when there's a purpose; God led me to share this sooner rather than later, and you'll understand why by the end!

Imagine thriving and arriving in your career of nineteen years, literally starting at the bottom, excelling through the business, climbing up the corporate ladder, and breaking those glass ceilings. There were times I would sit in a meeting surrounded by glass windows from the forty-fifth floor, and no one looked like me. I was the only Black female in those meetings.

I was often told by the senior leadership team I ran my retail stores like a well-oiled machine. When you walked in the front door, there was an aura of positive energy that exuded across the sales floor. My brain was needed—at least, that is what I was told by my director. I continued to excel throughout the sales organization. I was presented with an array of accolades such as highly effective performance rating; the leader of innovation; the best in class for my customer experience, grit, and tenacity; and went to a celebratory Circle of Success Winner luncheon as a finalist one year and nominee the next year at corporate. As I was writing this book, I stumbled across a gift card that was given to me personally by the senior VP. She handed it to me at a leadership meeting and it read, "For all you have done and continue to do to make the flagship store such as great success—we thank you, with gratitude."

I didn't mention any of those accolades to boast or brag, Instead, I mentioned them because I'm giving you a lesson. I'm painting the picture with my very own paintbrush. "You are your biggest investment. Take care of you because a job will get rid of you without hesitation as if you never existed. I've quit five jobs. I've given a two weeks' notice each time. I was let go each time before the two weeks were up. The moral of the story is we are all replaceable. Does your employer really care about you? Is the extra work worth it? Is the mandated overtime worth it? We are all disposable. Go home and spend time with your family. Use your vacation time.

Take a mental health day. Hit the gym. Make time for your physical health, hobbies, interests, passions, and personal development. Make time to live your life. We can't get our time back." (Howard, 2019)

I did this by God's grace and mercy. I suffered silently in a great deal of pain every day, but one thing's for sure; I showed up mentally my best self. I kept pushing to maintain that beast mode status I was known for by my track record, and I prided myself within the workplace. My work ethic was untouchable and meant the world to me. I always wanted to do a great job. I would mentor various employees through the years and often say to them, "We don't do mediocre work around here." I **never** complained; no one knew the physical pain I was going through.

God then said, "I have a new plan for you." I heard it clearly. He gave me this message for the readers.

I questioned, *What does that mean?* Well, I soon found out.

The unimaginable happened; I had a serious medical emergency, no more ignoring the physical pain, to the point my doctor took me out of work and the paperwork said "disabled." Yes, disabled, but I knew my God was able. Can you imagine being full of life, at the pinnacle of your career, and having no control over what was happening to you physically? I haven't worked in two years due to my physical disability.

It was God's way of saying, "I'm going to slow you down to get your attention to where I need you because you're not listening and you're moving too fast." I really wasn't listening;

I was career driven and all I knew was the job needed me. As a result, I continued to push until I was no longer able to do so. God also said, "I'm going to take care of you through this entire process, but you must be obedient." I'm doing my part, so He has kept His promises every single step of this journey.

Now, as you can imagine, this was a very traumatic experience for me. I've worked since I was fourteen. At that time in 2019, I just turned forty-seven and you mean to tell me I have to sit down for a minute? God spoke to me again: "Yes, you've done your work in a corporation." Still not really knowing what that meant, I questioned, "What do you mean?" He said, "I need you." I still didn't really know what that meant, but I am a firm believer everything happens for a reason. This is where my grieving journey began.

Let me pause here and give you a few tips.

1. Every traumatic experience has a grieving process. Recognize it, respect it, and care for it. Never allow anyone to dictate the time you need to go through your process. If you haven't fully gone through your grieving process, you will not be completely healed on your journey.
2. You can choose how to handle the trauma. As for me, I chose grace and turned my pain into power. I was able to create my very own personal healing journey through inspiration, affirmations, wellness, and spreading kindness to the world by way of social media.
3. Take the time you need to heal. Expect to have emotions through the process but know how to identify those emotions and what you need to do to protect them. There are certain triggers that cause these emotions to flare up. As

for me, it was any mention of work. If I saw commercials, paperwork, social media, or company vehicles, because of my dedication to the corporation and my customers, I would receive several phone calls asking questions/for support relating to the business. I would get questions asking if I returned to work and receive random social media requests from colleagues.

I underwent a major back surgery in 2019 in an attempt to get control of my physical life. If you don't know the level of pain or damage associated with this type of pain, you would never understand the physical and emotional stress I would endure on a daily basis.

A few months later, no real change in my condition, which is a major deal on paper, but I was and am determined not to allow my circumstances to dictate how I show up in life, I will not allow my circumstances to steal my joy and energy. I would show to the world the passion inside of me that has excelled me through my entire career. You think I'm going to let a circumstance kill my vibe? Nope. My prayer is I'm helping someone as I continue to share my personal experience with an unfortunate situation beyond my control.

I am the founder of my personal Facebook group that was a start-up to the Total Mind Body and Soul Transformation. In this group, the idea was to start with a weight loss journey and no other real plan in place. I created this group in the late hour of February 25 because it was a nugget from God, using my God-given gift, talents, and experience through coaching people to lead a successful and purposeful life. God then spoke and directed me to expand from a small, intimate group on Facebook to sharing with the entire audience on my friends list.

Do you see? In the earlier stages of my trauma, I wanted to go on my personal journey in private. I gained strength to come back to the Facebook world. This occurred because I felt I wasn't alone and both women and men could use healing in the midst of a pandemic. God reminded me I wasn't alone; we all were experiencing some sort of trauma during this time, whether it was due to job loss, death of loved ones, or changes in the economy. Through a huge shake in the world, I started sharing techniques through thirty-day challenges that were labeled the mindset makeover challenge, self-care/self-empowerment challenge, giving back, and prayer—all of which were my weapons throughout my entire healing process. Look how God equipped me with armor to get me through what would've been devastating to many and then placed on my heart to share with the world—I was chosen for this!

To be fully transparent, I never took the time to fulfill my passion in the past because I wasn't balancing my work and home life. I was giving all of my energy and passion to the job, and while my outside appearance stayed on point, I was, in some cases, ignoring what my body was telling me on the inside.

I'm going to pause here and give you a few tips to help you lead a healthy work and home life balance:

1. Do not ignore your body for anyone, any job, or anything. You're only given one on this earth, so please take care of it.
2. Make sure you schedule and show up for all doctor's appointments.
3. Remember, you're only as good as your last day worked, so make time for you. Take mental health days, take just-because days, and take time to spend with your family.
4. It is imperative you create a healthy work-life balance.
5. Make time for your passion and personal development outside of your job. Then, when life throws you a curveball, you'll be able to catch it and throw it right back.

It wasn't the pandemic that caused me to care for self; God had been preparing me for many years. He got my attention and forced me to realign with myself in 2019 for what was ahead in 2020. He is so amazing. I've been home for almost two years and because of my upbringing in the Church, I knew where my help was coming from, and my faith was solid.

Now, you know part of my story and I emphasize **part** because I will share more as we navigate this journey. With the way the world is set up with so much turmoil resulting from health, finances, mental health struggles, and hate, this was a perfect time to leave an impact by creating hope for anyone who may be dealing with any type of traumatic experience. I am speaking from personal experience. What I shared was pressing for two reasons:

1. I had to be obedient and do what God said, and that was to help my people through inspiring, encouraging, and

empowering during a time when the world could use healing. He has given me the gift, along with the opportunity, to do exactly what he has asked of me.
2. Although there is a process to getting through a traumatic experience, I am healed mentally. It took some time, but I turned my personal pain into power by going through my process using my very own gift. Even during the time when I was writing this and reading it over and over again, it was part of the process and confirmation I was healed because before this, I would get extremely emotional. My friends, as you know, the human is full of emotions and remember, trauma comes with emotions, so it's normal. **"It's okay to not be okay."** Just don't get stuck in circumstances you have no control over. Instead, keep pushing forward. By God's grace and my self-love, I am definitely in a much better place.

There's no way I could bring this forth in efforts to help the world if I wasn't fixed, right? Even though I am healed, there are things that will trigger my emotions as a human being. However, I get to dictate how I respond. I remember those are just to test my strength, so as a result, I will claim **victory** each and every time.

Prayerfully, my story will help you navigate through these challenging times and serve as a reminder you are not alone. While every circumstance may be different for every individual, you get to choose your happiness, even through a traumatic experience. I did; that's why I am sharing my personal story. I created my very own healing process, and **no one can or will kill my vibe**!

Now that you've survived the storms, my prayer is healing for you! You see, survival is getting through, like barely making it. Healing is when you turn that pain into power and be the absolute best version of you! It's your season; keep going and never give up!

DISCLAIMER
This book is not meant to replace medical advice or a diagnosis from a doctor. This book includes practical advice supported by professional opinions along with real-life interviews. The purpose of this book is for educational and informational use only.

INTRODUCTION

"Character cannot be developed in ease and quiet. Only through experience of trial and suffering can the soul be strengthened, vision cleared, ambition inspired, and success achieved."

HELEN KELLER

It was the summer of 2019. I was sitting on my deck, where I spent the majority of my days gathering my thoughts, enjoying the sounds of nature, and feeling safe at home. I was on a medical leave from my job for the first time in my life.

The only time I ever missed work would be during scheduled days off, so I began to feel really **stuck**. Have you ever felt stuck? Just imagine being so full of life and energy and having that snatched away without warning because of a sudden chronic illness. That's exactly what happened to me. I was in constant pain, so I had an unsteady gait that made my walking limited due to fear of falling. Therefore, I was limited with my daily activities and things most people my age would engage in, so it was a bummer. I felt like the best place for me was to stay at home, where I felt safe.

While I was forced to sit down, I realized just how precious life is and you need to care for yourself at all times. I was trying to process all that was happening with my medical condition. I was also trying to identify ways I could inspire, encourage, and empower other adult men and women out in the world who may go through trials and tribulations from trauma, whether it be physical or emotional.

Even though I was going through a medical emergency and my limbs were compromised, my mindset remained powerful. Though these physical challenges existed, I refused to allow them to take control of my vibrant life. In order to help myself heal both physically and mentally to help others, I had to put in the work.

Have you ever found yourself caring for others so much you ignore your own needs? What about your job? I found myself doing just that with my health. I would find myself rescheduling doctor's appointments so I wouldn't miss days at work, hesitant to request days off due to the workload and expectations. Recent research suggests that can be healthy if you're doing it the proper way. Putting others first can be very good for you. It can promote your satisfaction with life, give your life meaning, help you cope with stress, and promote your development of other positive character strengths that enhance the quality of your life and relationships. But if putting others first is motivated by less healthy reasons, it loses these strong connections to positive life outcomes.

"There are needs in our families, extended families, congregations, and communities, as well as within our network of professional associations. Almost everyone needs connection to others and the opportunity to give and get support in the abnormal new normal of deep uncertainty and the fearful specter of a pandemic. As executive coaches, we think a lot about how to maximize mental health resources—that's a big part of what we do every day. So, how can you shore up your mental health and deepen your own emotional reservoir? We can't share with others a resource we lack ourselves. The critical starting point is to take our own mental health temperature. How am I doing? What will help me combat anxiety? Am I drinking, eating, sleeping, or crying too much? What do I need to do to stay connected?" (Humble and Johnson, 2020)

I was so obsessed with serving people even through my own personal storm. In this life, I encourage you to be kind, have love for people, create a work-life balance, and remember you can't pour from an empty glass.

I was beginning to make plans with my health professionals to get back the quality of my physical life so I could return to work. It was mid-August 2019 when I made my final decision to move forward with a major surgery, which was terrifying. In my case, it became the last resort to getting my health back on track. I went into this with high expectations because the statistics around the surgery were really great. A successful surgery would have a six- to eight-week recovery period with an 85 to 90 percent success rate. While not perfect, it seemed rather promising, so I jumped on it because all I wanted was to get back to what I was passionate about—my job.

Whenever you have to make really big decisions regarding your health, it's not just a simple "let's do this." It is important to weigh out all of your options, seek second opinions, and be the absolute best advocate for yourself. When it's time, you'll be ready and know you made the best decision possible.

As the months continued to pass by, the world was hit really hard by a pandemic, which sent us all into a state of shock and panic. Remember the days of no toilet paper, barely finding the essentials, and food being rationed in the grocery stores? A yearlong struggle with the COVID-19 pandemic has brought more headlines than we as a society—as well as the people writing those headlines—could really handle. There's been speculation, sadness, chaos, fear, isolation, data, and graphs—so many graphs. But one of the earliest headlines of the pandemic wasn't about any of that. It was about supply, the supply of one product in particular: toilet paper. This all created havoc because of empty shelves due to panic buying or inability to keep up due to ill workers who contracted the virus.

When the world shut down, you could hear the bells from the stock market ringing daily on almost every news channel. It seemed as though the economy was on the verge of crashing. Although the world stopped, nurses, doctors, emergency personnel, grocery store clerks, and public works crews, just to name a few, were suddenly our superheroes. As a result, the memories are forever etched in the brains of those who suffered through the devastation of an unheard-of virus that plagued the entire world called coronavirus, often referred to as COVID-19. (King, 2021)

During these unprecedented times, life changed dramatically for many of us, whether it be through job loss, homelessness, financial hardships, death of loved ones, mental illness, or unexpected health situations. In the midst of the pandemic, police brutality got out of control and as a result, there was civil unrest due to injustice in the communities. What stood out was we were all in this together. There was nothing you could do to pay your way out of the situation; everyone was impacted. We seemed to find comfort in the most powerful five words you could hear echo across the world: "We're all in this together." While that was true, we were impacted in many different ways.

Needless to say, in the midst of writing this book, the pandemic was plundering through the states, creating distress, unmasking underlying mental health issues, and regurgitating existing emotional behaviors that were well managed. "During June 24 through 30, 2020, US adults reported considerably elevated adverse mental health conditions associated with COVID-19. Younger adults, racial/ethnic minorities, essential workers, and unpaid adult caregivers reported having experienced disproportionately worse mental health outcomes, increased substance use, and elevated suicidal ideation. The public health response to the COVID-19 pandemic should increase intervention and prevention efforts to address associated mental health conditions. Community-level efforts, including health communication strategies, should prioritize young adults, racial/ethnic minorities, essential workers, and unpaid adult caregivers." (et al. 2020)

With all of the mayhem going on in the world that has caused additional emotional sensitivity, families losing loved ones, households losing jobs, and the toll on the essential workers hustling through the pandemic, it's time for a call to action, an assessment on individuals' mental health to see how these untimely situations have caused trauma and the overall impact to the public. In my personal experience, I reviewed the three types of trauma and identified I suffer from chronic trauma.

THREE TYPES OF TRAUMA

ACUTE:
Often associated with a single event that happens in an individual's life, acute trauma could come in the form of a car accident, natural disaster, a single event of abuse or assault, theft, witnessing a violent event, or an experience that threatens an individual's physical or emotional safety. Such incidents and experiences can have a lasting negative impact on one's psyche and the way they live their life if left untreated. Acute trauma is also sometimes connected with short-term post-traumatic stress disorder.

CHRONIC:
Chronic trauma results from exposure to multiple, chronic, and/or prolonged overwhelming traumatic events over an extended period of time. Examples may include undergoing treatment for illness, domestic violence, childhood abuse, sexual abuse, and exposure to war or combat situations. Chronic trauma can even be made up from several instances of acute traumas happening one after the other. As with acute trauma, leaving chronic trauma unresolved can have a long-term negative impact on the quality of one's life.

COMPLEX:
Complex trauma results from exposure to varied and multiple traumatic events or experiences, often within the context of an interpersonal relationship.

"Past traumas may have an especially powerful effect on our reactions to this pandemic. If you're a survivor of medical trauma, for example, it may have echoes of a life-threatening illness or injury you or a loved one faced. In fact, the fear and uncertainty we face from COVID-19 can be a trigger for *any* kind of previous trauma, such as accidents, assaults, or abuse—any horrifying event you experienced as unpredictable and uncontrollable." (Gillihan, 2020)

Thinking back, you're probably wishing you were prepared with a toolkit full of things that would create magic to make this all disappear and bring happiness back into your life, simply looking for some sort of calmness to pave a way to get you through the unprecedented times. Just think about those who were at a pinnacle time in life—preparing to start that business venture, making travel arrangements to take that vacation they had been waiting all their life for, or plans to tie the knot—and out of nowhere, those dreams were shattered or put on pause. It's just too much to grasp, especially dealing with all of this unheard-of turmoil surrounding us.

July 2020 was when I realized I needed to put this story out, along with my techniques that could help many adults get through difficult times. You will be amazed you can continue to lead a positive life through devastation. You can choose to show up in a positive light daily, regardless of what's happened to you.

"*Trauma* is the Greek word for 'wound.' Although the Greeks used the term only for physical injuries, nowadays, *trauma* is just as likely to refer to emotional wounds. We now know a *traumatic* event can leave psychological symptoms long after any physical injuries have healed. The psychological reaction to emotional trauma now has an established name: *post-traumatic stress disorder,* or PTSD. It usually occurs after an extremely stressful event, such as wartime combat, natural disaster, or sexual or physical abuse. Its symptoms include depression, anxiety, flashbacks, and recurring nightmares." (Merriam-Webster Online Dictionary, 2021)

Have you ever experienced trauma? If you did, when it hit you, did you immediately start blaming yourself? In that traumatic experience, have you ever felt anxiety, depression, betrayal, or humiliation? Did you get emotional at the sound of anything related to the trauma? These are normal reactions to trauma triggers, so if you're nodding your head "yes," you're not alone, and I can guarantee if you keep reading this book, you'll understand why I say that.

You're probably wondering, "What are trauma triggers?"

"There are many ways you can reexperience trauma and, as a result, feel triggered. When something happens that reminds you of the traumatic event, this is called a trigger or being triggered. You might not even be aware of what is happening; you just suddenly react, and you find yourself in the middle of something you don't understand. It is common to not even realize you're being triggered." (Fox, 2019)

I'll share with you some stories of individuals, including myself, who went through both physical and psychological traumatic experiences. While I was going through my own personal storm, the world was in the midst of a pandemic. You'll also learn how we survived and managed to move forward with life with a daily dose of resilience and some simple techniques.

You're probably thinking, *Oh goodness, how much money will I have to spend to create magic or happiness?* While some things do require money, there are many other ways to create magic and bring happiness into our lives for little to no money at all. This book is unique and was birthed from my traumatic experience. As a victim of trauma, I understand everyone's journey is different, and I kept that in mind. As I interviewed the characters, I encouraged them to take breaks to care for their emotions. I understood their bravery and the importance of helping others by sharing their truths. When you read through this book, you will see I have core values that are important when dealing with individuals.

I am compassionate, kind, and proven to be trustworthy by the characters who entrusted me to archive their stories, family, friends, and supporters.

It's not healthy to ignore the trauma triggers, especially if you want to move on with a happy life. Over the months, I created my very own process to heal mentally from my emotional trauma, and it didn't cost me a dime, just an investment in myself, which was well worth it. I was willing to put in the necessary effort, time, and energy to create daily habits that ultimately became a way of life that changed me for the better forever. A growth mindset and an understanding I refused to be paralyzed by my circumstances. I was ready to face my truth and share with the world to let others see trauma can attack anyone, but you don't have to be a victim.

Can you believe some people also believe or act as though they will never experience an unfortunate situation? I can tell you trauma is inevitable at some point or another in our lives. That leads me to ask, "Would you be prepared in the event you or someone very close to you experience death, an unexpected medical diagnosis, or even go broke in the midst of these situations?" Not only did I have to embrace the medical trauma that forced me to get around using my new accessory I would refer to as the obnoxious cane, but I also had to face the pandemic. All of this was untimely; however, I felt more prepared than most when it came to the pandemic. I had my own toolkit full of techniques. What if you could use coping mechanisms that would be universal? These coping skills would help you push forward and solve problems in your personal and professional life if you suffer from trauma.

FOUR STEPS TO COPING AFTER A TRAUMATIC EVENT
1. Give yourself time; it could take longer than you expect.
2. Self-care. Be consistent with caring for you.
3. Ask for support from a trusted source.
4. Be **kind** to yourself.

I am here to tell you those experiences can bring out the best in you if you focus on the positive instead of the problem. As a survivor of my own personal trauma, I can share with you there is power in your pain. If I didn't go through the traumatic experiences, I would've never found my **purpose**. I was able to write this book to serve others and found every keystroke of the manuscript was my lifeline to therapy. Although trauma never goes away, you will find strength you didn't know existed, but it's a mindset. Trauma does not discriminate; you never know when it will land at your front door. The best thing you could do for yourself is move forward. Life is a beautiful thing and worth living, so put in the necessary work to care for your overall wellbeing. If you or someone you know has gone through a traumatic experience and are looking to move forward on your healing journey, you will love this book. It will motivate you if you go in openminded and willing to learn from another person's perspective.

One of the reasons I wrote this book was to help others that may be going through traumatic experiences to self-reflect, problem solve and feel empowered. As I shared my healing process, I found it beneficial to write it out. As a result, I thought it would be profound to add reflection questions and a worksheet after each chapter to allow you to jot down and feel the emotions to bring healing, choose happiness, challenge yourself and encourage you to be intentional and live your life with purpose even after the trauma. When completing each chapter, take your time and reflect on how you want to transform from the caterpillar to the butterfly using these tools.

CHAPTER 1

MY DREAM JOB

"If you want to be successful in this world, you have to follow your passion, not a paycheck."

JEN WELTER

Over the past couple of years, my passion and perspective on people has changed in an even more positive way. I've been on my own inward journey from my personal experiences. I make every effort to be kind and show compassion to every individual I come in contact with because life is short and everyone is fighting a battle you never know about unless they tell you.

In April 2000, I was hired by one of the largest telecommunications companies in North America, and from the time I was hired, I had a game plan. At this time, I was twenty-seven years old with my mind made up and a plan to make a career at this corporation and eventually have a leadership role in the Ivory Towers. As we learn through experience, plans don't always go how we anticipate. I was hopeful and going to do everything in my power to live out my dream, which was to land a gig at "the top." Regardless of what my family and friends would often say regarding my job being my life, I was determined to be the hardest worker.

When we think of people who always end up successful, we often wonder about their process. They even get this done with all the other tasks and events life throws at them. In actuality, they know or learn how to create successful plans. There's a lot of preparing and planning, of course. As I mentioned earlier, sometimes things don't go exactly how we plan, but at least we have an idea of a path to get us to what we dream about. Like Zig Ziglar said, "If you can dream it, you can achieve it." How many of you actually believe you can plan and follow your dream job? (Ziglar, 2021)

"Start by doing what's necessary, then what's possible, and suddenly, you are doing the impossible."
ST. FRANCIS OF ASSISI (BRAINY QUOTE, 2021)

I will share with you six tips on how I landed my dream job. These tips are from my toolkit you can use to help you create your plan, and what's super cool is they are universal, which means you can also apply them to your everyday life. I use them when I am creating any type of plan, whether it's professional or personal.

With my plan in mind, I started as a call center customer service representative because those were the positions available. I stayed in this position for about nine months before deciding I had enough of the phone interactions because that wasn't part of my plan. However, I knew I had to start somewhere in order to make moves and get to where we're going.

It was soon thereafter I started searching the open position requisitions board so I could move into another area of the business. As I stood in the hallway by the cafeteria of my old job, I saw a position listed for a front counter rep, and I knew I could do that, so I applied. Within a couple of weeks, I landed the new gig.

This was the ideal position then because of my passion for providing an exceptional customer experience, so I felt that suited me well. It would give me the opportunity to display my passion and skills in a face-to-face setting, and I would have direct contact with the customer. *Yes,* I thought. I was so excited to jump right in and be the best customer service representative at the front counter so I could transition into my plan.

By February 2001, I knew right away my original plan was well on its way, so I had to continue working toward that goal of getting to the top. Things were going so well; I knew I would land into a leadership role.

I worked really hard and took on additional duties. There were even times I would volunteer to do a task or go to events most of my peers would frequently refuse. I would raise my hand every chance the opportunities were presented.

All of my efforts and accolades really paid off. Soon, I was promoted to a manager. I wasn't surprised because I was confident, I met all the requirements to fast-track my way to success.

Although I was eager to tackle yet another new role, I knew this wouldn't be a walk in the park. However, I was up for the challenge. Imagine being promoted to manager and leading a team where you were once a peer for many years. I remember receiving an email from a coworker stating, "Are you sure you want to do that? You're jumping out of one fire into another."

Yes, she had the nerve to send that in an email without congratulating me on my new job. Over the years, I've learned not to waste too much energy on others' opinions. Those types of comments motivated and pushed me to do a superb job just so the naysayers would have to rethink. I learned I could do anything I set my mind to. No job was too big or too small for me. I was on my way to my plan just by putting in the work.

I went on to my new role as the manager, expecting pure chaos, and that's exactly what I was presented with for the first year. This was motivation for me, my vision, and my go-above-and-beyond attitude. I wasn't interested in the title; my interest was to be the absolute best leader in the business.

Have you ever had a boss who reminded you of how you never wanted to be if given the opportunity? I wanted to set the example for the employees who had the same, if not better, aspirations. I was very well known as being a no-nonsense type of leader who handled the business like a well-oiled machine. It was only a matter of time before my last mission was right around the corner. I didn't know what I wanted to do in the Ivory Towers, but I knew that's where I was headed, and my desire, dedication, commitment, and leadership abilities were going to excel me to that place.

> *"Don't wait for opportunity—***create it.***"*
> GEORGE BERNARD SHAW (GOOD READS, 2021)

As the years went by, I decided I had maxed out at the front counter and was ready to move on to bigger and better things. I made a proposal to my director, and he was delighted to give me the opportunity. I moved to a larger location managing double the employees and multiple projects were thrown my way. This all happened within less than three months of me stepping into a new team and location. Why do you think this happened so quickly? I took the initiative, so as a result, it felt like I hit the jackpot and was on my way closer to that dream spot.

I never once complained; I just gathered my team and set expectations. As the months went by, we were running tons of pilot programs for this telecommunications company right in the beautifully polished store that sat in an upscale shopping center in Pennsylvania. The store was flooding on a daily basis with corporate executives, so much so it had gotten to the point appointments had to be made for the corporate visits because while we were the leading the way, we still had to meet monthly quotas.

After months of successful pilots in the flagship store, I wanted to create a development program with my team. This training would be extended to any other employees who were interested. So, I did just that. I created my very own program titled Building Your Brand. I told you anything I set my mind to, I would execute on the plan. Believe in yourself; you can achieve anything you set your mind to. There are no limits out there; the only limits are those you impose upon yourself. Dream, believe, and act. Identify what you truly want, how you want to live your life, and act. Start to create the life of your dreams. Start small, dream big, and don't ever give up. (Meah, 2016)

Working with a team of millennials, it was very important to keep their brains intrigued. When I created the program, it was to give the employees an opportunity to learn or brush up on their professional development skills, learn the dos and don'ts of social media, learn how to dress for success, write out individual development plans (IDPs), and give an opportunity to speak with the senior leadership team that was there for a panel discussion as part of my Building Your Brand. This developmental tactic was a huge success and nothing that was already in place for this particular area of the operation. During this segment, I hosted visitors from all over the company to be part of this day; it almost felt like I was being scouted into my dream spot at the Ivory Towers. I knew everyone was very impressed because the higher-ups said they had seen nothing like this before.

A month later, I landed that dream role I had been chasing from the start. It's true what they say about hard work paying off. My hard work paved the way and there was so much growth along the journey. The problem is we don't always know how, when, where, why, or what it's going to look like. But with hard work comes growth, in more ways than you can see in the moment. (Floyd, 2020)

I was offered a national operations position in the Ivory Towers of this corporation. I remember going through the phone interview process with the executive director and being questioned. I could hear the change in his tone as he prepared himself to ask me the big question. The question he was about to ask me was a huge expectation in this industry, especially in the corporate setting. He finally mustered up the nerve. "I noticed you didn't include your credentials on your resume. Did you leave them off?"

A little caught off guard, I managed to respond quickly. There was nothing to think about because I am a very firm believer in being honest, so I said, "No, I didn't leave them off. I don't have a degree, if that's what you're asking."

He immediately said, "Oh, that's no problem, I just wasn't sure if you left them off in error."

According to Tesla CEO Elon Musk during a conversation at the Satellite 2020 conference earlier this year, "Colleges are not for learning, but rather a place to have fun." Musk said you can learn anything online for free and noted billionaire moguls like Bill Gates and Oracle's Larry Ellison dropped out of college. Ideally, he added, you would have dropped out of school "and did something." (Akhtar, 2020)

I've always been very confident in my abilities, and I had proven just what I was capable of doing. He and my new director happened to be visitors of the Building Your Brand segment. In most cases, corporate America requires a college degree for any level position. I earned my spot from all the hard work I had put in over the years—raising my hand when others wouldn't, taking those sidestep gigs, and during that presentation where it felt like I was being scouted when I led the company through several pilot programs, which turned into successful new launches for the company.

I was very proud of many things I did. However, one stands out in my memory. The company was taking on a new product and service and my team was selected to pilot the entire corporation. We did it. When I say "we," I give the credit to my sales team because I wouldn't have been able to do it without them. This task required long hours, and we had to make lots of sacrifices in order to make this a huge success. As a result, I was nominated Circle of Success recipient and awarded the Leader of Innovation Award.

Not only did I land this national operations position, but this position was new, and I was the first leader to get it started from the ground up. As I prepared to accept my new position and move on to the Ivory Towers, I gave thanks to my team in the upscale store because if it wasn't for their support, it would've been impossible to fulfill my plan.

Employees crave recognition for a job well done. Let them know you value their contributions and they play a vital role in the organization. Even better, tell them exactly what it was they did to earn your praise. (Economy, 2014)

I can remember when I was promoted to corporate; the announcement happened during a meeting. I was so embarrassed because I never liked attention. So, I was already uncomfortable because this was mentioned, and I wasn't prepared to speak to the group of people. I knew I was in the company of people who didn't really have my best interest in their own insecurities. Whether we want to believe it or not, everyone will not be happy for you and your success. There are people who want you to be successful, but not if they believe you are moving ahead of them. It isn't always spoken, but you will be able to recognize through their actions when your progression becomes reality.

Some peers sitting in the same room never wished me well on my new gig after the announcement was made, and there were others who openly extended their well wishes. I was fine, it was something I was immune to. I had tough skin because it would happen so often. I've always been extremely confident in my abilities and self, and I knew I had worked really hard to climb the ladder to corporate, so I didn't focus on the negative energy and clapped really loudly for myself.

As I moved on, I thought, *My plan worked; I am climbing the corporate ladder and breaking those glass ceilings in 2018 we often hear about.* I sat in offices in the glass building and, in most cases, meetings with people who didn't look like me. Many times, I was the only woman, and more times than none, the only Black woman. I always kept my hair on point; in fact, oftentimes, I would get questions about my hairstyles. If I wore a long style one week and a short style another week, no one was able to relate to how that was so easily done.

A lot of times, individuals are intimidated in that type of setting. It was fine with me. With my personality, I have the ability to work well with whomever I come in contact with, and most importantly, I love all people.

A very popular thing at corporate was "Let's go for coffee" and then one of the first questions that would pop up would be, "What college did you go to?" I never allowed that to intimidate me. Instead, I leveraged off of what I was told frequently, the fact I was one of the most knowledgeable people in the glass towers. I had "field" experience, which was very rare. So, I would respond with much confidence, "I didn't." My response would often leave them with a puzzled look on their faces, so that would lead to the next question: "Well, how do you know your stuff?" "One word: **experience**," I would respond. "I've been with the company for several years and this is what I did on a daily basis."

I never once felt I was out of place because, again, I knew I had something they did not, and they needed. I helped them with their jobs even though they carried the "credentials." It was often a thought and stated on several occasions by field members when you're sitting up in the towers, decisions were being made without really knowing what was going on within the business. My knowledge and experience carried me a long way. That was the advantage that made me a valuable asset to the corporation I carried with me to the towers.

According to FlexJobs.com, Harvard Business School conducted a study and found 37 percent of employers rank experience as the most important qualification in an applicant, not educational attainment. As you know, most successful corporations operate off core values to achieve their success. We, too, as individuals, can operate utilizing our personal core values to achieve success using our experience. Core values from my toolkit are what led me to my Dream Job

Plan—my experience, dedication, commitment, and most of all, my leadership abilities.

Here are six steps of experience to landing that dream job, whether it be an internal promotion or getting ready for that new gig.

KEEP AN OPEN MIND
Don't limit yourself! Remain open to trying new things from different perspectives. We program our brains to only accept what we want. However, we tend to limit our mindset. When I started the job, I knew I had great customer experience skills, and at the time, the first offer for me was a call center customer service representative. Was this my dream position? No. Was I going to turn down the opportunity of landing a gig? No. However, I kept my mind open, and I was able to recognize, sometimes, it may require a sidestep to get to where you're trying to go.

Being openminded typically makes you more adaptable to a unique work environment and job, as well as other employees. According to Christina Lattimer with *People Development Magazine* in 2018, employers usually want to hire someone they can mold into the type of employee who fits well in their organizational culture.

DETERMINE YOUR "WHY"
Why was this your decision? When you understand your "why," you will be most successful at achieving your goals

because they are **purpose** driven. Anything with a **purpose** has a meaning, and you will find happiness and fulfillment.

"Statistically, it is proven goals in written form give you the best chance of goal success. Writing down your goal helps you to clarify exactly what you want to achieve, which helps you guide your daily actions toward goal achievement." (Pelta, 2020)

Write out your goals. I found if I put them on paper, I was more focused and driven to achieve them because it seemed real.

PLAN AND PREPARE
Strategize your plan, write it down, and make it clear. This will help you stay optimistic and motivated, even when things are going off course.

AGE IS JUST A NUMBER
You're never too old to reach your dream—I started at the company when I was twenty-seven years old and landed my dream spot when I was forty-six years old. Nineteen years and I made it; I never gave up! I applied my plan and my values and landed at the top. Today's society stresses the importance of economic success as a measure of accomplishment—those jobs that have a generous salary are thought of as prestigious enterprises, whereas equally noble professions, such as social work, the performing arts and teaching, which unfortunately do not pay as well, are considered common and average. I believe I will find more happiness in a job that

is satisfying to me than that is satisfying to society. (Sanin, 1990) Your career choice should be a personal fulfillment, not title- or paycheck-driven.

Society has us believing money and titles are the key to happiness. I challenge you to think: What happens when you no longer have that paycheck or that title is stripped? Are you still happy? Don't you want happiness? Well, of course you do; we all do.

FOLLOW YOUR PASSION
You'll find guaranteed happiness accomplishing more of what you love. Think about it; when you're doing what you love, you feel all warm and fuzzy doing it, right? I can remember in 2011, I made a big decision to step sideways, which was considered a lateral move into a role. That sidestep turned out to be one of the best steps I ever made; it was guiding me to my dream job. I didn't earn any additional money in my paycheck, and I was fine with that because I was much happier in that stage of my life. It put me closer to home with less of a commute, and ultimately, it made more sense because I was able to save more money due to less automobile and travel expenses.

CRANK UP YOUR NETWORKING AND COLLABORATING SKILLS
Get out of the mindset of cliques; they don't get you far. If you mix with different groups, you're bringing different minds together, which helps you cultivate better ideas.

These are guidelines that worked for me, so I am sharing them as guidelines. It is important to come up with a career plan, as it gives you confidence, direction, and an idea of your career preference. You try them to get started on your career path.

"Millennials are more than three times as likely to switch jobs than older generations," according to a recent poll by Gallup. "But with all the job-hopping going on, it can be difficult to craft a long-term career strategy." (Adkins, 2016)

A solid career plan is important as it can provide a roadmap for your future. This, in turn, helps you make informed choices about your current job situation as well as future career moves. A broader career plan is also important when it comes to helping you stay inspired. (Luthi, 2018)

REFLECTIONS:

PAIN TO POWER PLAN
Transformation starts with you.

EMOTIONAL:
Why is it important to be kind to everyone you meet? How does it apply in the workplace?

PHYSICAL:
What can you do to plan and prepare for your dream job?

MENTAL:
If you're looking to make a career out of your new job, why is it important to go into a job with an open mind?

PAIN TO POWER PLAN
Transformation starts with you!

Emotional

Physical

Mental

CHAPTER 2

MY PLAN VS. GOD'S PLAN

"Many are the plans in a person's heart, but it is the LORD's purpose that prevails." God's purpose will always prevail and be better than any plan man can think of.

PROVERBS 19:21, NEW INTERNATIONAL VERSION

I'll never forget the feeling when I landed my dream job. Almost every day, I would think, *I really* **made it,** *I finally got the big city job in the Ivory Towers.* I was so thrilled and nervous at the same time. I dominated what statistics dictate about potential over education when trying to **make it** to corporate America. With the experience, I had exactly what was needed to get the job done.

I was extremely proud of myself because it was my goal to be successful and keep pushing until I made it! Regardless of what I was facing, quitting was never in my bloodline, so I say, never give up. I decided to go forward, and nothing could stop me but me. Being transparent, there were times

I almost got in my own way. No matter how confident I was in my abilities, fear and doubt are real and can creep their way in if you're not careful. I constantly stalled my progress because I believed a "perfect" moment would come. I quickly realized there was no such thing, so I got out of the crowded space in my head. I latched onto an opportunity when it was presented. I took a chance, stepped out on **faith**, went for it, and now I am here! Otherwise, I would've been waiting a lifetime.

My friends, the only way you will know if you've made the right decision is by getting out of your comfort zone and acting to make that one step forward. In order to do any of that, you must have confidence in yourself, believe in yourself, and trust yourself in order to activate your faith.

Acting as the national operations manager for a start-up area of the retail aspect of the corporation was a humbling experience. Whenever I shared my responsibilities with my colleagues, they would get really excited, especially when I shared about traveling around the world to assist with getting brand-new stores set up. Although it was exciting, I had a huge fear of taking flights; however, I knew when accepting this gig 20 percent of the position would be traveling—again, tackling another fear to be of value and make sure I gave my best every day. "For God has not given us a spirit of fear, but of power, of love, and of a sound mind." (2 Timothy 1:7 New King James Version)

In life, we have to conquer fear head-on in order to get to our purpose. Months went by and the doors of several stores were flying open under my training and leadership. I was also responsible for overseeing the cash deposits and equipment inventory. The position was a huge responsibility I was qualified for based off my many years of retail experience and leading the way through innovation.

After several months of being in my planned "dream job," it was time for performance evaluation check-in. This was one of my favorite times because it I could identify areas of opportunity and showcase my hard work. At the end of the check-in session, according to the corporate scale, I received a "Highly Effective" performance rating and was told by my boss, the director of operations, "We wouldn't be able to make it without you. Keep up the great work." All of my hard work was really paying off, and I couldn't wait to do an even better job.

My forty-seventh birthday approached, so that meant vacation time. In the most joyous time for me, I discovered some excruciating pain causing a lot of discomfort in my lower extremities. My legs felt really heavy, like tree trunks with a tingling sensation, and my toes were numb. Thinking back, I noticed a really sharp pain prior, but thought it was no big deal. You can count on your body giving you warning signals when something isn't right. My advice is not to ignore when your body is speaking to you and instead seek medical attention. I had to learn the hard way my health should've been my number-one priority, but when it came to certain things, it was the job that had my full attention.

In my mind, I never had the time to go to my appointments because I had to give my best at work, but here, I felt I would be fine to make it to my appointment. The pain I was suffering was really bad and felt different, so I knew it was imperative to be seen by the doctor. My mind was made up; nothing and no one was going to stop me from getting to that appointment. To think, mentally, I felt so refreshed after the vacation, but physically, I was stricken by pain.

The agonizing pain didn't stop me from going back into work after the vacation ended. My boss arrived a little later that morning, as he often did. We greeted one another and chatted about the joyous time I had on vacation. After he got settled, I reminded him of the doctor's appointment scheduled for the upcoming Wednesday. The train schedule switches up, which wasn't uncommon due to work on the railroad tracks. Since that was my means of transportation daily to avoid the thirty-five-dollar parking garage fee, I had to adjust. He immediately said, "You just got back from vacation." I understood, but this was a scheduled doctor's appointment I couldn't afford to miss.

A few hours later, I got up from my desk to head to the restroom and that sharp pain hit in my lower extremities like before. Only this time, the sharp pain made me feel like I was going to fall to the floor. I grabbed onto the lockers in the middle of the floor and stood there as if nothing was wrong. I was that tough girl—never missed work or wanted to show physical pain, but all along, I suffered in silence.

Once I was able to regain my balance, I headed over to my desk. I decided I'd better let my boss know what happened. In order to have the discussion privately, he and I walked over to the conference room, and I detailed the symptoms. He said to get to the doctor because it wasn't normal. My boss was extremely nice and accommodating at that moment, which was comforting for me. He suggested I get an Uber back to Delaware and charge it to the company credit card. Although I had an upcoming appointment, I knew this was urgent and couldn't wait. While I was sitting there, I was almost in tears because of the anxiety of not knowing what was happening with my body, and I also didn't want to leave work. I recall later calling my friend, Marlene, and crying because I was scared, saying to her, "I don't know what's happening."

This seemed different, and all kinds of thoughts started racing through my mind. I knew I was a strong individual; however, when you've never been in this situation, your mind can wander, and you can go into a panic. I immediately contacted my boss to let her know I wouldn't be able to report to work the next day. I was being admitted. He said he figured that when he hadn't heard from me. His next response was, "Get well soon, Missy," as he would often call me jokingly, then he followed up with a text that read, "I **need you**, and your family needs you."

I was released from the hospital on Tuesday, April 16, and given instructions to follow up with my doctor, who told me to stay home an additional week. I informed my boss, at which time, he started discussing a particular report he wanted me to complete for a big meeting coming up the following Tuesday with the SVPs. I went into shock; I just got home from the hospital, been advised to stay home for a week, and in pain, and he still managed to overlook my medical situation and ask me about completing a report. I couldn't believe I was hearing correctly.

I had to be assertive and speak up for myself. Sometimes we fail to do that in fear of retaliation from a superior. I expressed my concern of him asking me to complete a report that was due the following Tuesday when I didn't even know how I was going to manage from day to day. I reminded him I never miss work so to please give me support while I figured out what was going on with my health. I felt it was so unfair to have to explain my situation because I had never missed work for any reason. So, at that point, I was dealing with a medical scare and the pressure of the job because the bubbly and caring boss he was in the beginning when he thought this was just a short-term situation quickly turned sour.

After my follow-up appointment, it was determined I needed more time off than originally anticipated. My legs were heavy, tingly, and numb, all an indication of potential nerve damage. My gait was unsteady, which meant I could lose balance at any time and harm myself. There was no way I could catch a train, let alone stand on a platform at the train station in my condition without putting my life at risk. One tilt forward or over on that platform would've done me in. Once again, I had to make that phone call to notify my boss of my return-to-work status. He was constantly checking my return-to-work status even though it was reported in the third-party system that was utilized by the company. However, out of courtesy, I would still provide the information because that was the expectation.

Weeks went by and I was still at home, feeling at a complete loss. I had been a manager in the business for several years, so I was familiar with how the process worked on the other end. I had never been the one in need of support. As the days went by, I received calls from the human resources department; in my experience, it was extremely odd the human resources director would call me to ask for my return-to-work status.

Again, all of this information was accessible to management via a third-party portal. I got really overwhelmed because I was at home dealing with an expected medical emergency, and now, the people I worked so hard for were giving me a hard time for absolutely no reason at all. When I say "no reason at all," I was on an approved medical leave of absence, which was short-term disability, all of which was within company guidelines and the Family and Medical Leave Act. I was 100 percent compliant with paperwork, doctor's visits, and checking in.

The chronic pain and unnecessary pressure eventually caused emotional distress. I was always available for people, always sharing a smile or a kind word, and willing to work long hours. I was dumbfounded because the only thing that changed was, I experienced an unforeseen medical emergency. As days would go by, I started feeling something change with me—not only physically, but emotionally.

I was very much in check with my emotional and physical states at all times, so I felt the decline; that's when I felt it was time for me to be on the receiving end of support. I wasn't getting it from the people I was giving it to in the workplace. My mother, brother, and a few very close friends were always supportive. I know some wouldn't be able to handle me in the emotional state I was in because they were so used to me as the strong person saving the world, and now I was the one who needed to be saved. Thank God I didn't look like what I was going through.

I sought counseling. I have to say the counselor wasn't a good fit, but it was an outlet. When you feel you need counseling, do your research. It's best to be paired with someone who understands your culture and is able to communicate in a relatable way. You have the right to decide if it's not working. Be your own advocate; don't be afraid to shop around. You can dislike them for any reason; don't settle like I did. I know its's their job to get family history; however, I had no prior history and made that clear through the intake documents I completed. If you don't get with the right fit, it can cause more frustration. I needed help with the onset of adjustment anxiety disorder to get me through the life event that just occurred in my life, not my family history.

Needless to say, I spent a short period with the counselor, which was all I needed at the time. If you ever feel you're stressed or experiencing anxiety and you need an outside party to talk with, never hesitate to do your research and get the help you need with a therapist or counselor. You can also find support groups in your area through your doctor's office or your local hospital. Never be embarrassed or ashamed; it could cost you your life.

The calls continued from the human resources director regarding my work status. Can you believe I received no support from my director or any member of leadership during my time on the approved medical leave? When you give your all to a job and are no longer able to give anymore, you are only as good as your last day worked.

I received one last call from the human resources director inquiring, "What do you want to do when you return back to work?" I was beyond puzzled nothing had changed because I was out due to medical reasons. I began to realize the job had no concern about how I, a stellar employee who had never missed work or took a medical leave, was feeling. They were only clearly concerned about how they were going to proceed with the business and their bottom line. It became very apparent in the anxiety-causing phone calls, which led me to seek counseling.

A lot of the uncertainty surrounding my job was due to the bizarre behavior from the HR director and lack of compassion from the leadership. One might say, "Why would you be surprised by their behavior? Employers don't really care about their employees." Well, I never would've believed that in a million years, especially after winning multiple awards and being scouted by the director.

Fast-forward—the diagnosis is in: severe cord compression, spinal stenosis in my lumbar spine, and severe spinal stenosis in my thoracic spine, all of which are directly related to the nerves, spine, and spinal cord. "Spinal stenosis is a narrowing of the spaces within your spine, which can put pressure on the nerves that travel through the spine. Spinal stenosis occurs most often in the lower back and the neck." (Mayo Clinic Staff, 2020) After dreading the idea of surgery, I was told it was the last resort. My main goal was to get back to the job because my boss needed me, and second, my quality of life. Isn't it baffling how we tend to put a job or people before our own needs? As you can see in the prior statement, I was there at some point in my life. However, once I got the support, which included my own healing journey, I had a determined mindset to never put a job before my own personal needs ever again.

Anyone who has gone through a surgery procedure, you will agree it takes time to get in with the surgeon because there is so many waiting in line. Yes, I was able to secure my surgery date for October 2019 and told it had a six- to eight-week recovery period. That would put me back to work around late December 2019. Although I was opposed to the surgery, I wanted to get back to the job and that quality of life I was missing.

I received a letter from the third-party vendor that handled all medical leave of absences. This letter was written differently than all the previous letters. There was a shorter window to respond so I thought, *Why the sense of urgency?* Although I was startled, I immediately responded to the request. There went my anxiety kicking in again. I was slightly apprehensive because of the tone of the human resources director's phone calls leading up to this letter. I thought, *I haven't done anything other than succumb to a serious medical condition. Before this condition that knocked me down, I was a rising star, Circle of Success nominee, and carried many other accolades. What happened? What was different? Oh, I was no longer valuable to the corporation.*

September 17, 2019, a poorly written letter was delivered to my home by UPS, but this time, directly from the employer. This rocked my entire world. It literally shook me to my core. It was delivered to my doorstep by the logistics company. Imagine being home alone and opening this letter to get the news, "You're fired as of September 18, 2019." The poorly written letter went on to outline **all** of the things I did right during my medical leave. How do you send me a letter that proved I remained compliant, yet I'm **fired** after being out a little over four months? At the end of the letter, it read, "You can come back once you feel better."

I did so much research on whether or not this was legal and even consulted with an expert. Here's what I found: "Don't fire an employee unless you are meeting face to face. How you fire an employee is incredibly important. Do not fire an employee using any electronic method—no emails, IMs, voicemails, or phone calls. Even a letter is inappropriate when you fire an employee. When you fire an employee, give them the courtesy you would extend to any human being. They deserve a face-to-face meeting. Nothing else works. For morale's sake, it's important to remember your other employees have long memories. Additionally, during this time of social media dominance, you should assume any dismissal will not remain a private matter." (O'Donnell, 2015)

"You will have created a scenario in which your remaining employees are afraid to trust you. Or worse, they trust you may harm them too." (Heathfield, 2021) One would think you would get a phone call at minimum from a member of leadership or even human resources. You would think a "prestigious" corporation would have more empathy for their employees. I am at home, ill, and not a soul knew to what extent nor even had the decency to call me.

The letter listed a "timeline summary" of all dates and the actions taken between myself and the third party who was responsible for handling their claims. Each item was a representation I was fully compliant while on short-term disability according to the company guidelines and the Americans with Disabilities Act (ADA). This act is for individuals with disabilities both seen and unseen. You're probably puzzled, wondering why this happened, right?

"Unfortunately, based on the above information, it appears there are no reasonable accommodations that would enable you to return to work at this time and your need for leave is extensive, ongoing, and indefinite in nature. The telecommunications company is unable to grant an indefinite leave and will be administratively separating your employment effective September 18, 2019. Notwithstanding this decision, please know you remain eligible for rehire. We invite you to apply for any open position at the company in the future. If you would like information on vacancies with our company, you may visit the website."

So, when I am better, I can return to the company. I can't make this stuff up. That wasn't clear to me at all because in my experience as a member of management with this corporation, I've seen employees on a medical leave for nine months and come back to a job. Getting canned—what a slap in the face and a punch to the gut. Humiliating to say the least. I'd been loyal to that company for nineteen years. I was a "rising star," according to the method utilized to measure leaders. I proudly led the company through several transitions, traveled across the world, provided extensive training to other employees, and rated at the very top for customer experience. As a result, I was tasked with leading a customer service training that was developed with another peer. I even led the company to launch brand-new services and products across the world. I was a key contributor in that corporation and their bottom line.

I named what I could to paint a picture to prove it doesn't matter who or what you were, but what matters is what you could do for them.

Wow, this is what I get for finally taking care of myself, was all I could think as I picked that letter up to make sure it was really happening. I couldn't believe it; they did not even have the decency to contact me by phone to know if I was alive. I would be dishonest if I said it didn't bother me. Thoughts of fear, humiliation, embarrassment, and betrayal raged inside of me; they hit me like a ton of bricks. I mustered up the strength to walk away gracefully.

In the end, it was a rewarding experience due to the valuable lessons I am able to apply in life and share with others. Trauma isn't universal. They are not death sentences, but instead a source of power to push you to your purpose. I had to get over the disbelief because it was very important for me to move forward. A month later, I learned the department I was working in was part of a realignment. Anyone in business can tell you a realignment doesn't happen overnight. I began connecting the dots and remembered a decision to fire someone, especially in my situation, had more to do with the company than the individual.

"Sometimes you need to get knocked down before you really figure out what your fight is, what you're fighting, and how you need to fight. Sometimes you need to feel the pain and sting of defeat. To activate the real passion and purpose God predestined inside of you, God says in Jeremiah, "I know the plans I have for you, plans to prosper you and not to harm you, plans to give you hope and a future." (Jeremiah 29:11, NIV). Hear me well; on this day when you have reached the hilltop and are deciding on next jobs, steps, careers, or further education, you will rather find purpose than a job or career. Purpose crosses disciplines. Purpose is an essential element of you. It is the reason you are on the planet at this particular time in history; your very existence is wrapped up in the things you are here to fulfill. Whatever you choose, remember, the struggles along the way are only meant to shape you for your purpose.

When God has something for you, it doesn't matter who stands against it. If it's meant for you, God will move someone who is holding you back away from a door and put someone there who will open it for you. I don't know what your future is, but if you're willing to take the harder way, the more complicated one, the one with more failures at first, the one that has ultimately proven to have more meaning more victory, and more glory than you will not regret it, press on with pride, press on with purpose, and appreciate what God has brought you through. (*ABOVE INSPIRATION*, 2018)

Here are three lessons I learned during this process, which you can apply to move forward after devastation.

GRIEVE THE LOSS/GROW THROUGH YOUR PROCESS

People don't get to decide your pain; only you are responsible for your process. In my experience, my job loss was huge. I put nineteen years of dedication, commitment, and undeniable loyalty. That hit really hard, like a ton of bricks. I didn't do anything; I was disabled, a condition that can spring up on any individual. The way I lost my job devastated me. At the same time, it was a sigh of relief because I knew they were up to something. Take the time you need to heal. It's your grieving process. When you're ready, move on, and embrace the new. You will see there is something beautiful waiting for you.

CREATE A WORK-LIFE BALANCE

The job and management do not care about you. It's about their bottom line and making business decisions. Regardless of how hard you work, no matter how loyal you are, no matter how many times you've worked longer hours than scheduled because they needed you, always do what's best for you and your family because they will replace you as if you never existed.

BE IN TOUCH WITH YOUR EMOTIONAL WELLBEING

If you feel you need a counselor/therapist, seek professional guidance to assist you with getting your emotions back on track. It could just be a matter of talking to someone outside of your circle. A lot of times, our circles tell us what we want to hear or the load is too heavy for them to handle. To be clear, speaking with a therapist/counselor doesn't necessarily mean you need medication—just an outlet. I'll be sharing from my toolkit throughout the book; don't miss out on the opportunity to take care of yourself.

I didn't expect a chronic illness and never in a lifetime did I expect to be fired from my dream job. However, I've learned a ton of valuable lessons that have made me more attentive to my personal needs, vulnerable, and more in tune with myself. I would've never written this book if they didn't fire me.

When God has a plan over your life, it doesn't matter what your plan is; He will make you uncomfortable because something drastic has to occur to make you move. In this case, He fired me because I would've never moved onto my purpose. I thought because that was my plan and I was an exceptional employee, I would've been in that industry until I was ready to leave at retirement. God's plan over my life is much bigger and unfolding, and that is helping others in a way He wants. God said my time expired in the corporation; it was just the foundation adding to my experience.

REFLECTIONS:

PAIN TO POWER PLAN
Transformation starts with you.

EMOTIONAL:
Did you make a plan to commit to a work-life balance?

PHYSICAL:
What can you do to ensure your health is your number-one priority and still do your job?

MENTAL:
When you go through a traumatic experience, how can you position your thought process to understand God always has a plan for your life that's designed better than you could ever imagine? Once your mindset is stable, how can you prepare yourself to receive it and wait on it?

PAIN TO POWER PLAN
Transformation starts with you!

Emotional

Physical

Mental

CHAPTER 3

BETRAYAL

"I never knew how strong I was until I had to forgive someone who wasn't sorry and accept an apology I never received."

UNKNOWN

That day I was on the receiving end of a workplace betrayal was shameful. I never imagined being hurt by a place I dedicated years of my life to. When you're loyal to your job or a relationship, the magnitude of hurt or distrust could feel the same. In my situation, I learned a valuable lesson I will carry with me for the rest of my life and would like to share with you. Never give your all to a job so much you forget about your life, because at the end of the day, you are just a number. The harm can be disturbing.

Betrayal can be paralyzing if you allow it to be. You have to understand when things happen to you, they serve as a lesson or a blessing. Life goes on with or without the individual or individuals who betrayed you. I was reminded by my brother and a great friend it was their loss. It took me a second to grasp what was being said, but I thought they were right. I was more than "just" an employee. It wasn't my fault for what happened.

"What do you do when you discover the person you've built your life around never existed? When 'it could never happen to me' *does* happen to you?" (Waite, 2017) How could the man who wanted to marry you so badly, have you to keep and to hold until death do you part, shatter your entire world without early warning signs?

In an interview with Rose, she shared her experience with betrayal from her estranged husband. Rose is a beautiful and vibrant forty-seven-year-old entrepreneur and program manager by day. She has a beautiful daughter and son-in-law. They graced her with two grandsons and later with a grand princess who you will learn became such a blessing to the family. Rose adores those grandbabies and would do whatever necessary to support the parents.

Rose was living the life in her beautiful five-bedroom home and felt her life was complete. She was married to her second husband who she often referred to as her "forever." They would take trips around the world together and do all sorts of fun stuff happily married couples did together, such as laugh, celebrate, have fun together, and be physically affectionate.

In this marriage, Rose was the breadwinner of the household for a period due to her "forever" quitting his job to fulfill his dreams of entrepreneurship. In this new age, one would frown upon the idea of the wife carrying the household; however, that was no big deal for Rose because she felt it was best for their marriage and she was willing to carry the load regardless of what society thought. Whatever he wanted, she was supportive of her "forever's" big ideas.

As the years went by, there were no signs of trouble—until that dark day in August 2018. The love of her life hit Rose with a bombshell. Rose will never forget the day he walked into their warm kitchen and said, "I no longer want a title, or to be married. I no longer want to be a husband."

"You no longer want to be married?" said Rose, trying to maintain her composure. She walked off, thinking to herself in disbelief, *did he just say he no longer wanted to be married? And without an explanation?*

"We were happy," said Rose. "We had a blissful marriage. We just purchased this five-bedroom home with intentions to extend our family. How was this possible?"

She received no answers and didn't understand why all of this was happening. Her world shattered.

The day ended and there was still no rhyme or reason to the sudden news. Rose was scheduled to leave and spend two weeks with her grandchildren, primarily to help out with the newborn, when he hit her with this news. She was distraught and had no clue where to turn. She questioned, "How is this happening? I thought we were extremely happy."

She was so frazzled by the unexpected news she started to cancel her flight to Florida. However, the "forever" convinced her "to just go ahead on the trip and when you return in two weeks, we can talk." Although she didn't want to leave because of the devastation and not knowing what was next, Rose took his advice and headed out as planned.

"Can you believe this guy didn't want to communicate for the entire two weeks I was away?" said Rose. Due to the chain of unexpected events, Rose traveled to Florida with a heavy heart and her mind on the marriage that seemed to be disintegrating without warning. She kept this from everyone for an entire two weeks because she was embarrassed. Can you imagine the emotions that were raging internally? She went through a period of anger, embarrassment, being and emotionally drained. By God's grace, the grand princess became her "superstar." In fact, she gave her the nickname of "superstar." The grand princess employed so much joy in her life at the perfect time. God has a way of taking care of his children by putting the right situations or people in our space at the right time.

While our acts of betrayal came from a different source, I can remember a time when I felt a sting from betrayal and all of those exact feelings rushing through my mind, body, and soul. In my experience, I was the same way; I didn't want anyone to know what I was going through. In hindsight, I wanted to understand I couldn't feel in embarrassed because I didn't do anything wrong. I shared with Rose what came to mind during the interview. I deduced society is so judgmental and we as human beings fear being talked or thought about negatively. Rose agreed and we both realized, in our experiences, we were able to get beyond those feelings by changing how we processed what other people thought about us. After going through our process, we realized what others think of us is none of our business. Much like how

Rose found joy in visiting with her "superstar," I found joy in my personal toolkit.

We all react to trauma in different ways, experiencing a wide range of physical and emotional reactions. According to a February 2020 HelpGuide article, Emotional and Psychological Trauma written by Lawrence Robinson, Melinda Smith, MA, and Jeanne Segal, PhD, there is no "right" or "wrong" way to think, feel, or respond, so don't judge your own reactions or those of other people. Your responses are **normal** reactions to **abnormal** events. In my personal experience, when going through betrayal, I felt shock, denial, disbelief, confusion, fear, guilt, and shame, and I wanted to be alone for a period. Here are some signs to look for according to the HelpGuide article.

SYMPTOMS OF PSYCHOLOGICAL TRAUMA
Emotional and psychological symptoms:

- Shock, denial, or disbelief
- Confusion and difficulty concentrating
- Anger, irritability, and mood swings
- Anxiety and fear
- Guilt, shame, and self-blame
- Withdrawing from others
- Feeling sad or hopeless
- Feeling disconnected or numb

Physical symptoms:

- Insomnia or nightmares
- Fatigue
- Being startled easily
- Difficulty concentrating
- Racing heartbeat
- Edginess and agitation
- Aches and pains
- Muscle tension

Rose was on an emotional roller coaster, experiencing anxiety, sadness, and disconnection due to the news her husband hit her with before heading off to Florida. Her new granddaughter brought so much joy into her life at a time when she needed it most. During her time away, she had so much time to reflect on her marriage, yet still had no answers from the "forever" regarding the bombshell he hit her with. Rose's trip ended so she headed back home on the dreaded four-hour flight. The anticipation of knowing more had really kicked in. Her senses became more open, and she paid more attention to the little things her "forever" would do. Rose arrived through the front door of their beautiful home, placed her bags down, and sat to have a heart-to-heart regarding the bombshell so she could move on with her life. The "forever" had a new habit of hiding his phone. Rose was bewildered by all the changes and was still trying to piece together what triggered the "I don't want a title anymore."

She came across some disturbing images in the "forever's" cellphone of the same sex, so she tried to get information and piece the puzzle together. The "forever" denied the interactions between him and the other male.

She spoke up and said, "It is over. I can't compete with another man."

He assured her nothing was happening and changed the narrative, saying, "You're blowing this whole thing out of proportion." He wanted to work on their marriage. As the wife who thought she had her "forever," she accepted his story because she wanted her marriage to last.

Although Rose knew what she saw on that phone that night, she blocked it all out of her mind because she was willing to save her marriage. She wanted to work on her marriage so much she suggested marriage counseling of, which he was opposed to.

Life went on as a "happily" married couple. He eventually agreed to try counseling, although he only attended one session. This was a huge step in the right direction to get their marriage back on track. They were looking forward to their annual Christmas party and began making plans. Things were going great and back to "normal."

What Rose didn't know was three months later, her world would completely fall apart and there would be no picking up the pieces. She discovered her husband's betrayal in a way no woman would ever want to experience.

November 29, 2018, was a normal day for Rose and the "forever." They followed their morning routine of kisses before walking out the door. He called her throughout the day, so nothing seemed unusual. What she didn't know was it would be her last day kissing him goodbye.

The workday ended for Rose, so she hustled to the train as part of the weekly routine. As she approached the train, she sent a text to the hubby asking, "What would you like for dinner?" What was bizarre that day was he didn't want anything for dinner. He told her not to worry about cooking. Rose said, "Okay, I'll just pick up something on the way home."

Rose arrived in the driveway and walked into the front door of the beautiful five-bedroom home. She was on the phone chatting with her best friend, Sunny. She placed the dinner on the island in the kitchen and noticed the mailbox key was there. That seemed odd because they had their own keys. As she walked around the kitchen, still on the phone, she opened up the coat closet and saw it was empty. She went to check one of the bedrooms upstairs and noticed an empty room.

"Oh my god, he's really gone," she said to Sunny. Still in disbelief and shock, she sat down to regain her composure so she could read the text he just sent. The text read, "So we're officially separated." He took his belongings, moved out, and sent a gut-wrenching text—a total disregard of the now ex's feelings and her broken heart. Although all the signs were present, she still wanted to believe this wasn't really happening.

An hour passed by, and she was still waiting for a response. She ran downstairs to the big window and noticed there were no cars in the driveway. She thought, *The "forever" got what he wanted.*

Rose realized she was a victim of abandonment by her estranged husband. He borrowed enough time from the conversation in August to get himself together. Even after she realized, there was a sense of disbelief, so she ran to the security camera and played back the chain of events for that day to see how it played out. It was all there in color. A U-Haul truck backed up in the driveway of the upscale neighborhood garage. She couldn't believe her eyes, but it was there in plain sight. The warning signs were present all along. She just didn't want to believe the man she married, the same one who gazed into her eyes at that wedding when they said their vows, would have the guts to cause so much pain. To put the icing on the cake, he left for another man. He was a coward! He wanted to live his "other" life right in front of Rose and did not have enough respect to tell her the truth.

The one thing Rose could hold on to was she knew she was an excellent wife. His demons were bigger than the marriage and he deceived Rose for many years. She was sitting alone, distraught in the living room. She felt weak and betrayed and didn't know what she was going to do with the five-bedroom mortgage. However, she knew she had a great support system with her mother and a few select friends. What was a little different, though, was Rose was always the "strong" one helping her family and friends. Now she was the one who needed help. That can be intimidating for loved ones if they're not accustomed to helping others. If individuals aren't equipped to provide emotional support and are always on the receiving end, they may feel a little uncomfortable. Rose's friends were able to jump right in and give her what she needed, though.

God gave Rose warning signs her "forever" wasn't what he was pretending to be. She suspected that as well because he would always put on an image for his friends. In her mind, she knew he was fabricating his life. We tend to look beyond those red flags when we're in love or want to believe the best and give individuals the benefit of the doubt. She started recanting all of the evidence that was laid out for her and thought, *Wow, the evidence was here all along.* She just didn't want to believe it. Outside of the bombshell in August, there were the photos of estranged's male lover in the cellphone and an electric bill in the estranged's name that showed up in Rose's email.

Rose questioned, "Why would an electric bill come in his name for another address?" She nonchalantly let her husband at the time know about the email and he brushed it off, saying it was probably spam or fraud. She told him he should check into it because someone may have stolen his identity. What Rose found out later was the estranged moved less than three miles away from their home. Rose said she "felt like she was living in a scene of a Lifetime movie titled *Husband Walks Away from His Wife.*"

When God has a plan over your life, sometimes he has to make things drastic to get your attention. He wanted her to see she deserved so much better and the estranged was never meant to be her "forever." Rose spoke to the estranged's aunt to inform her of what had taken place and the aunt said, "The day he walked out, God was there." She knew this as well, but she had to get through the gut-wrenching feeling of losing what she thought was her "forever."

Rose realized life must go on, so she started her healing process. She recalled it was ugly in the beginning, but she knew God was going to turn her ashes into beauty. We have to go through a process of healing during any traumatic situation in order to heal. She said she would get up in the mornings, stand in the mirror, and ask God, "When are you going to take the tears away?" She said she didn't sleep for thirty-six hours straight. She would try to pray herself to sleep every night.

One of her girlfriends, who is a licensed clinical social worker, said to her, "You're going to have to drink some Sleepytime tea. You've got to allow your body to rest because you're on an adrenaline high." She wasn't doing anything, and that included not taking in any food because she was focused on what transpired. As a result, she lost six pounds in three days.

Rose would go to work every day, smiling on the outside, but on the inside, her heart was in pieces. Rose would dress up for work, put on her "whole armor of God," and literally recite the scripture every day. (Ephesians 6:10–20, ESV)

Rose remembered her estranged would buy her gifts, but they never would be what she wanted; instead, they were what he wanted her to have. She was scheduled to go Christmas shopping in New York with him, but since they were estranged, she went with her mother and girlfriends. She wanted to treat herself to a Louis Vuitton bag; however, she realized all of the expenses she had to undertake due to the circumstances, so she decided not to get the bag after all. Even though she felt she deserved it, she knew she had to be more responsible because of the bills the estranged left her with to figure out on her own.

Rose would grab her Bible and turn to the "whole armor of God." It was a powerful scripture that helped her get through her dark days. When she was feeling low, that was her defense. As we know, this may not apply to your experience with betrayal; however, it's a start to getting your life back on track. In my opinion, if you're wearing the full armor of God, you have nothing to worry about. His protection will supersede any battle meant to destroy you.

THE WHOLE ARMOR OF GOD

"Finally, be strong in the Lord and in the strength of His might. Put on the whole armor of God, that you may be able to stand against the schemes of the devil. For we do not wrestle against flesh and blood, but against the rulers, against the authorities, against the cosmic powers over this present darkness, against the spiritual forces of evil in the heavenly places. Therefore, take up the whole armor of God, that you may be able to withstand in the evil day, and having done all, to stand firm. Stand therefore, having fastened on the belt of truth, and having put on the breastplate of righteousness, and, as shoes for your feet, having put on the readiness given by the gospel of peace. In all circumstances, take up the shield of faith, with which you can extinguish all the flaming darts of the evil one; and take the helmet of salvation, and the sword of the Spirit, which is the word of God, praying at all times in the Spirit, with all prayer and supplication. To that end, keep alert with all perseverance, making supplication for all the saints, and also for me, that words may be given to me in opening my mouth boldly to proclaim the mystery of the gospel, for which I am an ambassador in chains, that I may declare it boldly, as I ought to speak." (Ephesians, 6:10–20 NKJV)

The process to recovery is not a one-size-fits-all, but these are some techniques Rose used to pull through and they could help you take the first step into moving forward.

ANGER

You've been hurt by someone you cared for and planned to be with forever. You may want to retaliate by causing harm to the individual(s). There were nights Rose wanted to get out of her bed and drive the three miles to the estranged's apartment to key his car, flatten the tires, or bust all the windows. Rose wanted to inflict some sort of pain on him because of what she was going through. Never is this a productive act and it will typically cause more harm to you than even the situation itself. Find ways to contain your anger. Rose would sit down alone and go through photos of them and cut them to pieces each time she found herself in the state of anger.

"Learn the lesson. Whenever a betrayal happens, what remains is an opportunity for deep personal growth. For this transformation to begin, though, you must be willing to open yourself up to the possibility there is a lesson. It is critical to drop the defense mechanisms, such as blame and guilt, because as long as you are pointing a finger at the other person or yourself, it will impede your ability to learn. The lesson might be to trust your gut and not override your first impressions. Or the lesson may be there are kind people in the world who support you when you feel you lost everything. And if you choose to forgive the other person, never forget the lesson. Betrayal will feel like your world is falling apart. However, healing is possible and building healthy emotional skills will help you plan for your next best steps." (Meekhof, 2019)

ARMOR OF FRIENDS IN YOUR CIRCLE

It is important to have a circle of family and friends when you're in a time of need. "Psychologists and other mental health professionals often talk about having a strong social support network. When trying to reach our goals or deal with a crisis, experts frequently implore people to lean on their friends and family for support. Social support can be gestures that are supported by family and friends such as lending a hand if they're unable to financially support themselves as a result of a traumatic situation, sit with them if they need someone just to listen and maybe step in and be an advocate at their doctors' appointments if they're unable to fully understand what is going on with their health condition. Research has also demonstrated the link between social relationships and many different aspects of health and wellness. Poor social support has been linked to depression and loneliness, altering brain function, and increasing the risk of the following: (Cherry, 2020)

- Alcohol use
- Cardiovascular disease
- Depression

- Suicide

Rose encourages anyone going through a rough patch in life to make sure you have a great support system. Surround yourself with people who will encourage you and pray for you. Rose and I both found there is power in prayer; it will cause things to shift. She had about four friends who were there every step of the way, and it made a huge difference in the healing process.

JOURNALING

When you go through a traumatic experience, writing about it can be very therapeutic and help heal your mind, body, and soul of the stress. "Make lemonade out of life's lemons. Lutgendorf notes people who are able to find positive meaning in traumatic life events enjoy better health than those missing this perspective. It doesn't mean what happened was good; it may have been truly awful. Still, it's well established those who experience trauma and adversity often become stronger and more resilient. If you train yourself to watch for the positive that emerges out of negative (or even devastating) events, it positively impacts your mind and body" (Haas, 2019). Rose sure did make lemonade out of the lemons with her journaling. Her writing consisted of daily letters to God.

In the end, Rose moved on with her life, sold the five-bedroom home, and lived better than she did when she was married. It took this experience to uncover the fantasy life and there is more to happiness. God gave her the soil and planted Rose in her new life. Just like her name, she has blossomed into a beautiful rose.

Anyone who's suffered from betrayal should be assured they have the courage, strength, and vulnerability to transform, resurrect, and reclaim yourself. It's not your fault, but it is your fate. (Meekhof, 2019)

REFLECTIONS:

PAIN TO POWER PLAN
Transformation starts with you.

EMOTIONAL:
Have you ever been in a situation (work, relationship, family member) where you felt betrayed? I know forgiveness is a big step; however, it's for you. Have you forgiven the person and moved on?

PHYSICAL:
What did the betrayal feel like?

MENTAL:
If you were able to move forward, what was your process? If not, how can you work to move forward after reading this chapter?

PAIN TO POWER PLAN

Transformation starts with you!

Emotional

Physical

Mental

CHAPTER 4

THE PROCESS OF GRIEF

No weapon formed against you shall prosper, and every tongue which rises against you in judgment You shall condemn. This is the heritage of the servants of the Lord, and their righteousness is from Me." says the Lord.

ISAIAH 54:17 NEW KING JAMES VERSION

Grief is one of the most difficult emotions for people to deal with and can be devastating. Most people associate grief only with death of a person. Respectfully, I do understand how one would feel that way. In my experience, I equate grief with mourning. Any time there is a loss of something you were connected to, we can refer to it as dead. This happens as you go through emotional turmoil after being exposed to any traumatic situation. According to a 2016 Mayo Clinic article, "Grief is a strong, sometimes overwhelming emotion for people, regardless of whether their sadness stems from the loss of a loved one or a terminal diagnosis they or someone they love have received.

"They might find themselves feeling numb and removed from daily life, unable to carry on with regular duties while saddled with their sense of loss.

"Grief is the natural reaction to loss. Grief is both a universal and personal experience. Individual experiences of grief vary and are influenced by the nature of the loss. Some examples of loss include the death of a loved one, the ending of an important relationship, job loss, loss through theft, or the loss of independence through disability.

"Experts advise those grieving to realize they can't control the process and to prepare for varying stages of grief. Understanding why they're suffering can help, as can talking to others and trying to resolve issues that cause significant emotional pain, such as feeling guilty for a loved one's death.

"Mourning can last for months or years. Generally, pain is tempered as time passes and as the bereaved adapts to life without a loved one, to the news of a terminal diagnosis, or to the realization someone they love may die. If you're uncertain about whether your grieving process is normal, consult your healthcare professional. Outside help is sometimes beneficial to people trying to recover and adjust to a death or diagnosis of a terminal illness."

As we've learned from the experts, trauma can be a loss of a job, a divorce, an unexpected health situation, and so forth. Grief is the process you grow through during your most vulnerable moments. Due to the painful emotions that come with grief—such as fear, anxiety, depression, guilt, anger, pain—grief can destroy you if you let it. When you allow yourself the right to heal, there is an upward end of grief. There is potential to grow, focus, and experience acceptance and hope if you allow yourself to.

My personal advice as you grow through your trauma and the grieving process: take time for you. In your time of caring for yourself, it is important to not overwhelm yourself with the circumstance, but instead to focus on your healing journey. Since there's no way to put a timestamp on grief, remember to be patient with yourself as you go through the process. Although almost every person will experience some sort of trauma in their lifetime, most outside people will not be able to understand your grief, let alone your desired process. My friend, it's not meant for them to understand. However, it is crucial for you to recognize, respect, and care for yourself. People are insensitive to sensitive matters unless they have encountered an unfortunate situation.

The process of grieving is not a one-size-fits-all, but some techniques from my toolkit pulled me through my mourning of the job loss and unexpected news of my chronic illness. It's possible they can help you take the first step in moving forward. If they don't interest you after you've tried them, then at least you're getting a better idea of what will work for you on your personal journey.

MAKE SELF-CARE YOUR #PRIORITY

When we think of self-care, we primarily think about all the vain things, but it goes beyond that. Remove the barriers in your mind and open up to things like prayer, yoga, meditation, journaling, exercise, and creating a powerful music playlist. When you create your playlist, fill it with a variety of genres that will be well suited for whatever phase you are in at that moment. I say "that moment" because your grieving process can change from time to time. It gets a little deeper, too—remove whatever is causing you additional stress. Are you overextending yourself? Don't be afraid to say **no**; set boundaries.

PROTECT YOUR SPACE
It is possible to live a meaningful and fulfilled life even beyond the person you were before your traumatic experience. In order to do so, you have to protect your space. Eliminating anything or anyone that doesn't bring **joy** is a way for you to experience peace after the loss; it's a form of protecting your space. You have full control of your emotions and how you respond to anything or anyone that shows up to disrupt your peace. At the end of the day, you're the decisionmaker of what and who belongs in those categories.

KNOW WHEN YOU NEED HELP
Refer to your "tribe," those who are there and will handle you with care during your most vulnerable moments. It is important to understand everyone isn't equipped to help you with your heaviness. In other words, they may only want to hear the initial trauma when it occurred. You know that person who may say or think, "Girl/Boy, you still talking about that?" Well, of course you are, because you're still mourning. In order for you to fully grieve and release the loss, you may need to talk about the situation multiple times. Don't be afraid to seek support from a third party that has experience

with grief trauma. In my own personal experience, I had a few friends I could share my truth with and then there was a part they weren't able to handle so I sought a counselor for a short period.

My personal advice: do whatever sets your soul on fire to help pull you out of devastation. Uplift yourself on a daily basis. Getting yourself out of a dark place does require work, but you are more than worth it, so start by identifying what works for you and what makes you happy. For example, taking walks in the park can be therapeutic. According to a December 2021 *Sports Medicine* article, Can Physical Activity Support Grief Outcomes in Individuals Who Have Been Bereaved: A Systematic Review by Angel Chater, Julia Zakrzewski-Fruer, Gillian W. Shorter, and Jane Williams, in 2018, there were 616,014 registered deaths in the United Kingdom (UK). Grief is a natural consequence. Many mental health concerns, which can be identified as grief outcomes (e.g., anxiety and depression) in those who have experienced a bereavement, can be improved through physical activity. The exercise was paired with alone time, reading your favorite book, and sitting on the beach. When you're on the beach, it's like you're away from the world and in tune with the sounds of nature, flowing to the rhythm of the waves when you hear them crashing against the sand. It is such a serene experience.

It is powerful to visit with support groups because you will get the opportunity to connect with others who are going through grief as well. It allows you to release your emotions in a safe place. Alone time is frowned upon; however, it is essential as long as you know when. Society has made everyone believe we must do things that require you to be in a relationship or in groups of people. The norm is to want to do things with friends, spouses, and family. I agree with a close-knit support system during your time of grief.

Give yourself permission to step out of your comfort zone and into unfamiliar territory. Allow yourself space to get quiet with just you. I know you're probably thinking, *Why would I step into unfamiliar territory during such time in my life? Isn't this when I need people the most?* "When I went through a breakup a few years ago, what helped me the most wasn't ice cream or vodka. It was spinning. When I awoke before dawn during those first raw months with an overwhelming ache in my gut, I somehow managed to drag myself and my misery to a 6:30 a.m. class, and by 7:15 a.m., I felt confident I could get through the rest of the day. Yes, I was pumped on endorphins and Beyoncé. But there was something transformative about all those sprints and climbs. Sweating—at least as far as I could tell—was healing my broken heart." (Richards, 2014)

In my experience, there is so much power in doing all of these things. When you get familiar with yourself, you will learn things you didn't know. This is where your strength will flourish.

Grieving doesn't have a time limit. Some get through the process faster than others, recognize it, respect it, and care for it. One of the most empowering things for me was all the times I identified my triggers and knew exactly how to get beyond them. The power of healing is the day you can celebrate by burying those triggers. My advice is to recognize, respect, and care for your situation, and each time you are able to do one more thing than you were before, celebrate with what makes you happy. As I demonstrated above, your self-care doesn't have to always be associated with money, but instead something small that soothes your soul and lets you know you are moving forward on your journey.

As you grow, the trauma still exists; you just learn how to navigate and not be a victim of your circumstances.

Life will throw another curveball just when you think you've gotten over a particular phase of your grieving or mourning journey. "For instance, it is normal for a person to go through an extended period of isolation, loneliness, and depression months after the initial loss. What feels like an abnormality is, in fact, perfectly healthy when dealing with grief." (Hawkins, 2017) Those trigger points will rear their ugly heads again. Like when I was fired; I felt the pain internally. However, because I was equipped, I pulled one of my self-care tips out of my back pocket and turned what was trying to destroy me into a positive.

My stomach would turn to a point I felt nauseous when those "Facebook memories" I posted when I was in the pinnacle state of my career would pop up. I climbed the corporate ladder and "broke glass ceilings." I would get that pit in my stomach because it was painful. I would scroll past them so quickly. It wasn't until I allowed myself to go through my grieving process that I would begin getting stronger and stronger.

As the days and months went by, I utilized my healing process from my toolkit to help pull me through. I would clear my mind by stepping back and viewing those memories through a positive lens. So instead of feeling down, I flipped it and reminded myself of just who I was then and still am. Once I did that, I found myself creating self-help videos to encourage others who were going through rough times and feeling a pit in their stomach. That gave me the strength to continue viewing each one of them.

I was notorious for throwing a positive spin and wasn't afraid to show the world. I wanted them to see it's perfectly fine to grieve, go through your process, and continue to make memories so you can look back and remember exactly the power you held, and nothing and no one can take that from you.

While we all grieve differently and have different reasons for why we are experiencing grief, you are not alone on your journey! There is hope to stabilize your emotions and live beyond the circumstance. "It is okay to feel pain. It is okay to feel scared. It is okay to feel uncertain. It is okay to feel grief. It is okay to feel lonely. It is okay to not be okay. Yes, it will pass. Yes, it is impermanent. But you can honor your emotional experience by being present for it, not by distracting yourself or avoiding it with every fiber of your being. Just for today, show up for whatever you're feeling." (Rose, 2019)

As you grow through your grief, embrace the pain, and learn to not blame yourself for what's happening to you. Access the trauma and practice gratitude by looking around at all of the things that are going well in life. It's not over. "From my own experiences with loss, as well as those of thousands of grieving people I have companioned over the years, I have learned you cannot go around the pain of your grief. Instead, you must open to the pain. You must acknowledge the inevitability of the pain. You must gently embrace the pain. You must honor the pain. As crazy as it may sound, your pain is the key that opens your heart and ushers you on your way to healing.

"Honoring means recognizing the value of respecting. It is not instinctive to see grief and the need to openly mourn as something to honor, yet the capacity to love requires mourning. To honor your grief is not self-destructive or harmful; it is self-sustaining and life-giving." (Wolfet, 2016)

"I can be changed by what happens to me, but I refuse to be reduced by it."
                                    MAYA ANGELOU (GOOD READS, 2021)

REFLECTIONS:

PAIN TO POWER PLAN
Transformation starts with you.

EMOTIONAL:
Pain is normal. Have you tried any coping skills to help ease the pain? If so, what were they? Try jotting down a few from the list above.

PHYSICAL:
Do you get enough rest?

MENTAL:
What are some ways you can process grief so you're not overwhelmed with emotions?

PAIN TO POWER PLAN

Transformation starts with you!

- Emotional
- Physical
- Mental

CHAPTER 5

BROKEN BUT NOT FORGOTTEN

"Broken crayons still color."

DAVID WEAVER

April is a fifty-five-year-old educator with over twenty-eight years of teaching experience. April is passionate about her craft, full of life, and loves reading, writing, and spending time with her husband, daughters, and grandchildren. April was an advocate of doing your own breast examinations at home, as encouraged by gynecologists all over the world. The end of September 2018, after performing her own breast self-examination, she identified a lump in her breast, so the sign was there. To be sure, she asked her husband if he felt the lump. He said, "Yes." So, she was confident the unthinkable was happening to her.

April recalls reporting it immediately to her doctor. "When it comes to early detection, regularly examining how your breasts look and feeling for abnormalities is crucial. In fact, women often discover many problems themselves first. And the earlier you find breast cancer, the better! In addition to going for mammograms and annual check-ups, experts recommend all adult women—beginning at age eighteen—perform monthly breast self-exams to check for lumps and other changes that might indicate the presence of breast cancer.

"Continue the practice of giving yourself a breast self-exam throughout your life, even during pregnancy and after you go through menopause. Performing breast self-exams on a set, regular schedule will help you notice when things don't look or feel quite right." (Logan Sport Memorial Hospital, 2021)

April had a few Bible verses she lived by; this was one of them: "Wisdom is the principal thing: therefore, get wisdom and *in all thy getting, get understanding!*" (Proverbs 4:7 KJV) It was then April received devastating news in October 2018 she wasn't ready to accept—it was confirmed she was diagnosed with breast cancer at the age of fifty-three. We all wish we could be prepared for the unexpected. As soon as she received the diagnosis, all sorts of thoughts wandered through her head. April even shared she felt so embarrassed and ashamed she didn't want anyone to find out about her cancer diagnosis other than her husband, mother, and her boss, and that's where she wanted it to stay.

April went through a surge of emotional trauma, which is totally understandable. She was angry, and she began to blame herself as if she stood in a cancer line and invited this horrible disease into her life.

"A cancer diagnosis can throw a person and their loved ones into emotional turmoil. It's perfectly normal for anyone diagnosed with cancer to go through a whole range of emotions, often several in a day. Coping with cancer can be as difficult emotionally as it is physically, and those feelings may continue through treatment and even years after recovery." (Henderson, 2017)

She recounted in her head the family members and coworkers who were diagnosed with cancer, and she started to compare what she would potentially experience with what they went through. April soon realized everyone's experience was unique to them; no two treatments would be the same. After she began to digest what was happening, she realized she had to learn how to move forward with life. While she knew her emotions were triggers from the diagnosis and she was an emotional wreck. She began to feel better as she remembered how the Lord always brought her through her most difficult moments. She had to learn to stand strong and mighty in the midst of the storm. She remembered she is a child of God and was often referred to as a warrior by all of her close girlfriends and family members.

April had to remind herself, "I **am** God's property, He has greater plans purposed for me!" It was those words April held onto, never forgetting her faith. So, she decided to pray and talk to God, telling Him she didn't want anyone else to know. She needed his guidance. She thought about her children and tears began to pour. How was she going to break the news to them, especially since her oldest daughter was expecting her first baby? April's embarrassment of the situation held her hostage until she prayed to the Lord. She wanted to keep it from outsiders, but God spoke to April and reminded her if she would open up and share with others, there would be more people to join her in prayer for a complete healing. At that moment, she moved aside for God to navigate the healing process.

After her encounter with God, she felt comfort and relief and begin sharing her story with others. She was still self-conscious about her circumstances because the more she spoke about her breast cancer diagnosis, the more questions she got from people. As a result, it was like she kept reliving the trauma. April decided to wait until it was time for her medical leave to share with her coworkers and colleagues. She didn't want to deal with the questions and rehashing the emotional pain. At that point, April asked for her coworkers to respect her privacy as well as keep her in prayer during her surgery and healing process.

April had a mastectomy in December 2018. According to a 2019 Mayo Clinic article by the Mayo Clinic staff, a mastectomy is a surgery to remove all breast tissue from the breast to treat or prevent breast cancer. After her mastectomy, April was very hesitant about going through with the chemotherapy because of the horror stories she had read about through her research, as well as information shared by her coworkers who had gone through the process. She was so afraid she found herself fighting the process. April's husband, Casey, whom she labeled as her hero, was the wind beneath her wings. He stood in the gap, asked her oncologist questions on her behalf, and was extremely supportive. Her husband told her if the chemo was needed, he would support her through the entire process. Her youngest daughter, Jazmyn, was in

Turkey in the Air Force at the time and attempted to come home but wasn't allowed leave time. April's oldest daughter, Acasia, was in Spain with her Navy officer husband. She was eight months pregnant and couldn't travel at that time.

April decided to move forward with the chemotherapy treatments, still not knowing what to expect. However due to the health crisis she was experiencing as a result of the breast cancer, she knew it was necessary for her healing journey. April had to endure twelve rounds of chemotherapy a week and radiation treatments every day for five long weeks. Chemotherapy started January 2019 and lasted through March 2019. Her radiation treatments began in May and concluded June 2019. April wasn't prepared for the side effects. She knew she would potentially lose her hair; however, she didn't expect the nausea; loss of appetite; skin discoloration; weight loss; dark, brittle fingernails; fatigue; memory loss; and runny nose. April said, "Even long after, there are lasting effects such as neuropathy."

As time progressed, during her chemotherapy treatments, April dealt with extreme bouts of depression. She returned to work January 2019 with two days off during the work week. She needed that time to deal with the impact of chemo on her body. She prayed and eventually decided she needed to do something to bring herself out of that state of helplessness and depression. She realized though she could not control her situation, she had control of creating a positive change for herself and others.

She began to think about breast cancer survivors and warriors who were in the same predicament and who had overcome. As a result, April started an amazing breast cancer campaign through BreastCancer.org.

Because of the loss of all of her hair and return to work, she began to wear scarves on her head. Realizing others were impacted by this dreadful disease, she felt a need to do something fun and meaningful with the headwraps, hats, and scarves. She invited family, friends, coworkers, and even the medical staff where she was getting her treatments to join her efforts to support and encourage others. April called her breast cancer fundraiser "**Rock Your Scarf/Hat.**" Her sister-in-law, who is a breast cancer survivor, introduced her to doing research on breast cancer awareness. April was relentless as she started doing personal research and getting involved in support groups with people who were going through the same illness. That all lifted her spirits and helped her pull through the depression that was creeping into her life from her traumatic medical diagnosis.

When you're going through traumatic experiences, whether they be health or emotional, there will be times you want to be alone; however, from my personal experience, I highly recommend support groups. According to an August 2020 Mayo Clinic article, Support groups: Make connections, get help by Mayo Clinic staff, "Support groups bring together people who are going through or have gone through similar experiences. For example, this common ground might be cancer, chronic medical conditions, addiction, bereavement, or caregiving. A support group provides an opportunity for people to share personal experiences and feelings, coping strategies, or firsthand information about diseases or treatments."

The breast cancer campaign created by April, "**Rock Your Scarf/Hat**," was a huge success and well received in the breast cancer community. At the end of her final chemo treatment in March, April invited everyone to wear scarves and hats. The hats were to make everyone feel comfortable because they had lost their hair through the treatment period. By this time April had returned to work, so she wore her scarf and hat. Her personnel were supportive and even allowed her to do a project one day where she invited all of the staff to share with them her experience and educate them on what she had learned from her personal experience. April said, "It was one of the best things that came out of the trauma, along with the experience I was able to share with others."

April got herself prepared for her final chemo session. She went in as she normally would at the nurse's station. After some time passed, her nervous energy started kicking in, so she played around on her phone while waiting for the nurses. April said, "This was routine for me in an effort to take my mind off of the process." It was something different about this visit because they were taking longer than usual. Talk about uneasy; she had no idea of why it was taking so long because it was a typical chemo day.

Unbeknownst to April, they were intentionally stalling to set up her table for what was going to be one of the most exciting times of her life. The charge nurse from her chemo had contacted the media department. Not only was she eager to return to work, but the nursing team prepared a special event because of the breast cancer awareness fundraiser she hosted. April could barely control her emotions because they thought enough of her to take time out of their day to make it a special moment. The media guy showed up with his camera and several people in the hospital rallied around April to give her an opportunity to speak about her campaign.

The banger was April's article was published and landed in the hospital newsletter along with her beautiful picture on the front cover. This was an exciting ordeal she never would've considered being a part of if it wasn't for the breast cancer diagnosis. As April went through her emotional and physical wounds, she still managed to find ways to support others who were dealing with the same type of traumatic experience.

As we know, the "C" word doesn't show up as rainbows and sunshine. April started in a dark place, like a dark hole, but she had God, hope, inspiration, and faith that guided her, and as a result, she no longer suffered from depression and is proud to say today, she has been breast cancer-free and a survivor for two and half years. April had one last step after treatment—plastic surgery, which she underwent in February of 2021. Although April suffered with depression for a period, she was often called a "warrior" because she was able to withstand all the pricks, tugs, and pulls to her body and go on with life daily.

While she has successfully completed the treatments and is in remission, her body is riddled with chronic pain, along with neuropathy, on a daily basis. However, she manages to move forward because she was grateful to survive through that experience.

During our interview, April said, "I would like to encourage all individuals to do self-examinations at home, schedule your mammograms as prescribed by your physicians, and do your research so you can understand the medical terminology the medical professions use. It is critical so you can understand what is specific to your diagnosis. Be the best advocate for yourself!"

Share only with someone you can trust because this is your body and your diagnosis, so you have to protect it and you. Please ask questions and go to your doctor's appointments prepared with a list of well-thought-out questions; it is your right as a patient/survivor. Think about how many times you leave the doctor's office and remember something very important you forgot to ask at the appointment. That list will save you unnecessary stress. It is your life at stake, so use your voice. This applies to all of your medical visits to the doctor, not just a medical diagnosis visit.

In addition, April came to terms with her depression and realized the breast cancer was a medical diagnosis; it wasn't the end. In her case, she won the battle. April said one of her favorite scriptures would play over in her mind. God was greater than her circumstances. "His Grace is sufficient and He will supply all of your needs." (2 Corinthians 12:9, NIV)

It's amazing in the midst of April's storm, she focused on the breast cancer campaign to give to others while getting her mind off of the situation. She felt that was God's way of taking the lens off her pity party and resetting her energy to do something within her scope of control.

When life seems to be spiraling out of control, let God's word anchor you in place. Mind the Bible for His promises to you and let these words become the very foundation of your days. When things get darker or more chaotic, repeat these scriptures to remind yourself of the reality of the situation and see things from His perspective. Remember that:

- **He is in control and is stronger than your problems:** "In this world, you will have trouble. But take heart! I have overcome the world." (John 16:33 NIV)
- **He loves you and has plans to prosper you:** "For I know the plans I have for you, declares the Lord, plans to prosper you and not to harm you, plans to give you hope and a future." (Jeremiah 29:11 NIV)
- **He works all things together for good in your life, including what you're going through now:** "And we know in all things, God works for the good of those who love Him, who have been called according to His purpose." (Romans 8:28 NIV)
- **He will give you the strength you need to get through the storm:** "So do not fear, for I am with you; do not be dismayed, for I am your God. I will strengthen you and help you; I will uphold you with my righteous right hand." (Isaiah 41:10 NIV)
- **His timing is perfect:** "There is a time for everything, and a season for every activity under the heavens." (Ecclesiastes 3:1 NIV)
- **He never leaves your side:** "The Lord is near to all who call on Him, to all who call on Him in truth. He fulfills the desires of those who fear Him; He hears their cry and saves them." (Psalm 145: 18-19 NIV)

April explained how life isn't the same after a cancer diagnosis. She learned life takes on a different perspective and changes who you are as an individual. "After a marathon of breast cancer diagnosis and treatment that may last six months to a year, you can hardly wait to get back to a normal life again. But the day of your last radiation treatment or chemotherapy infusion doesn't mark the end of your journey with breast cancer. Instead, you're about to embark on another leg of the trip. This one is all about adjusting to life as a breast cancer survivor. In many ways, it will be like the life you had before, but in other ways, it will be very different. Call it your "new normal." (Shaw, 2021)

April said, "It was a reminder life can be short and it was easy for me to trust God." April was grateful for her husband, her mother, her children, and her circle of family and friends. She strongly recommends joining support groups, as they give you a sense of community.

To anyone going through a diagnosis, don't be afraid to ask for help. Regardless of how strong you feel you might be, we all need help at some point in our lives. Those who care for you will be right there to lift you up when you fall. Follow the instructions of your healthcare provider and take note from April. She is a thriving breast cancer survivor, and hopefully you see it is possible to live many years beyond the diagnosis. Don't allow the diagnosis to stop you from going out and living life to the fullest. Take those walks in the park and catch those flights around the world if you desire. In the next chapter, you will get to learn about why we go through different challenges in life. Some may be surprised to learn the science behind our struggles.

REFLECTIONS:

PAIN TO POWER PLAN
Transformation starts with you.

EMOTIONAL:
"Breast cancer" is one of the most devastating things a woman can hear. If you're in this situation or any disturbing health-related situation, what can you do to care for your emotions?

PHYSICAL:
What will you do to keep an eye on your breast changes as a measure of early detection or possible prevention?

MENTAL:
How will you control your thoughts when faced with devastating news?

PAIN TO POWER PLAN

Transformation starts with you!

Emotional

Physical

Mental

CHAPTER 6

THE PURPOSE OF ADVERSITY

And we know that all things work together for good to them that love God, to them who are the called according to His purpose.
ROMANS 8:28, KING JAMES VERSION

Adversity: a state or instance of serious or continued difficulty or misfortune. (Merriam Webster, 2021)

Have you ever had a well-thought-out plan? I did when I finally got the dream job I worked relentlessly to achieve. With so many aspirations, I hit the ground running with several wins in the first six months; then, out of nowhere, due to a medical illness, that dream job became a nightmare. That day, September 18, 2019, was the day my job was snatched away and will stay forever in my memory. My life changed forever, but I was determined to be set **free** from everything out of my control. I had the power to turn those lemons into lemonade, but it all depended on my self-determination. That was my opportunity to reinvent myself and I had all the necessary tools. As you've witnessed from my experience, I was living my dream and my world came crashing down due to uncontrollable circumstances. This can happen to anyone at any time and can be extremely hard to prepare for.

"Life is going to challenge you at some point. It's going to hand you something unfair. It's going to take something from you. It's going to interfere with your plans. When this happens, you have a few choices. **Deny, cope,** or **thrive.**" (TED, 2015)

Yes, life can be brutal and hit hard without notice, a blow that knocks the wind out of you. It can have you gasping for air, as if it's your last breath. Imagine not being able to breathe, your life flashing before you. When life hits us the hardest, that knockout you didn't see coming is when you feel it the most. One thing about life is it will not discriminate. If it's your turn, it's your turn. Be ready to decide whether you're going to put on your body armor and take the blow like a champ or succumb to the knockout. Get up off the floor, evaluate what just happened to you, and make some serious decisions.

Before you take your next step, the question is, "Will I push forward, or will I just lay down waiting for someone to breathe life back into me?" When you're lying there, it can seem unfair, thoughts running through your mind as you question, "Why is this happening?" When I went through my misfortune, I didn't wait or gather around for a pity party; I put on my body armor, fought for my life, and ended up leading the pack.

I would like to reflect a little over my story from Chapters One and Two. I was at a pinnacle state in my career and landed a spot in corporate America, a place where so many only dreamed of getting to. Although I was silently suffering, I would pack my bags in an instant to catch a flight to support a troubling store. After my return, I would share with my boss I had to request for airport assistance to push me in a wheelchair to get from one end of the airport to the other. I also remember the times we had meetings a block away from the corporate office, I would catch an Uber due to the pain. At one meeting, my boss laughed at me for catching the Uber a block away. I never once complained; I did what I had to do to get my job done.

Oftentimes, I would be embarrassed catching an Uber for a short distance, but I had no other choice. Every day, trucking from the office to the train platform, I would take a break by stopping and rummaging through my bags as if I was looking for something. That was just to get a break and relieve the pressure from my back and legs. People tend to look down on people with disabilities and even more so on unseen disabilities.

When I use the term "suffer silently," I mean you look great on the outside but are physically hurting. If you suffer from chronic pain, depending on the impacted area(s), your mobility and strength may be limited. As for my pain, I dealt with all of the above. They never go away—tingly toes, thighs too sensitive to touch, numbness in my legs, foot drop, afraid you may trip and fall in certain settings, and just overall being uncomfortable.

All sorts of questions were running through my mind. I went from several MRIs and EMGs that left blood on the white sheet of the examination room bed. The physician's report said I was disabled and my condition, if worsened, could cause paralysis. It was so scary to hear this news and the fate of my job. I so badly wanted to get back to work; however, in order to do so, I had to regain the quality of my life. I made one of the scariest decisions ever—to proceed with surgery.

I did all the right things to maintain my job, but I was fired. Once I was able to digest what was happening to me, I still didn't quite understand why. I was determined to do something about my life, and it wasn't to be crippled with depression or anxiety. I had to retrain my brain to think positively because I knew God had other plans for me based off what He whispered to me that one day: "Your time is up here." I wouldn't lack anything. I was unsure of what that meant; however, fired was the last thought. I spoke a lot about customer experience because I thought if I put it into the universe, He would put me there. It may be hard for some to digest that every trial or tribulation serves a purpose that's meant to strengthen us to allow us to grow. To this day, I believe God fired me so I could take the step and walk in my **purpose**.

One might would ask, "Why would God cause something bad to happen?" I was one of those people until I became a witness to His many blessings and realized in order for me to get in touch with my purpose, something drastic had to occur. Remember, it was my dream job, and I was comfortable navigating within the company.

I can't lie—it was tough when it initially happened. I felt my vibrant life was ahead of me and was excited about my new gig. In my opinion, things were going well. Even with the pain I was suffering, my focus was the job, so all was good even while my health was failing. As the days went by, I said, "Ah ha, I see you, God. This is what you're doing in my life, and this is why certain things had to happen."

"Does it seem like every challenge you experience becomes a big headache in your life? No matter what adverse events you are currently experiencing, there is a purpose behind each one. For most of us, it's difficult to imagine losing a child or finding out you have cancer is a blessing. I know from personal experience. I was sexually molested and exploited at the age of eighteen. It took me a while to view it as a learning experience. The way in which you view adversity will either allow you to be set free from the heartache, confusion, guilt, and fear or allow you to be negatively affected in every aspect of your life." (Mason, 2014)

September 2020, in the midst of the pandemic, God spoke to me and said, "I want you to help my people." I didn't really know what that meant at first, so I began listening during my morning prayer time. He said, "I want you to do exactly what you've been doing on social media but expand it to everyone." In order to fully understand or hear what God is trying to communicate, you must quiet your mind and remove outside distractions.

Here is a Bible verse to consider when listening to God:

"Then a great and powerful wind tore the mountains apart and shattered the rocks before the Lord, but the Lord was not in the wind. After the wind, there was an earthquake, but the Lord was not in the earthquake. After the earthquake came a fire, but the Lord was not in the fire. And after the fire came a gentle whisper. When Elijah heard it, he pulled his cloak over his face and went out and stood at the mouth of the cave." (1 Kings 19:11-13 NIV)

"Notice God's voice came to Elijah as a *gentle whisper*. We have to be quiet to hear a whisper." (Klinge, 2018)

I created an intimate Facebook group on February 25, 2020, with about seventy-five people that focused on living a healthier lifestyle, inspiring, encouraging, and empowering others. In the midst of my storm, I created a group to help others; that was ultimately my healing place. I needed accountability to keep me focused on my healthier lifestyle and I wanted to be kind to others to heal my own wounds of betrayal as I faced adversity. Isn't it amazing how God will use His people as vessels to get a point across to people in need? He was using me in just that way. I would get so many private messages or shoutouts from members in the group of how I was changing their lives. This was confirmation God fired me to get me to my purpose.

In my time of adversity, I learned a lot of lessons about how being vulnerable was important so people would realize they weren't alone, being transparent, putting your faith in God, and being kind to everyone regardless of what they've done to you. I thought, *Wow, God gave me everything I needed for this platform through my experience at the corporation.* It was like He was setting the stage and it was time for me to go into action. I am very shy and never want the spotlight on me, but I also knew I was bold, confident, courageous, and passionate enough to do whatever He wanted when it came to connecting to His people. So why not take His guidance and step out on faith during a time when the world was going through oppression and challenge?

I was extremely afraid because that would require me to let down my guard, but I could see others were hurting and could use my strength. "My hill isn't that different from yours—the adversity, challenges, changes, and obstacles we face on a daily basis or suddenly appear in our lives. You can't afford to surrender, because the cost of doing so is nothing less than your goals and dreams. Obstacles, whether they are people, objects, or situations, can always be overcome. There is always a way when you don't compromise the standards you set for yourself and never give up!" (Saunders, 2021)

As a young kid, I grew up in the Church, so I had the required fundamentals; however, I am not as well versed on the Bible as I should be, so I would often lean on my brother, Antoine, and my sister-in-law, Michele, for a good scripture. I would often reach out to them and say, "Can you give me the most powerful scripture?" They never disappointed; they would always come through and go the extra step by breaking it down. My purpose was to familiarize myself in this assignment God sent me on, I would cover many topics I could use from personal experience to connect with His people as He requested and help people who were not as knowledgeable.

As the months went by, God would resource me with all types of messages without having to prepare. I remember walking in the park, creating videos for social media, and my best friend, Larnelle, would say, "Are you free styling?" I would chuckle and say, "Yes." She would then say, "You and that big head. Where do you come up with all of this stuff?" That was confirmation I was walking in my purpose and everything that happened to me in 2019 was a blessing. God was doing exactly what He promised—providing me with everything I needed.

In April 2019, that sharp pain hit my lower back and went down my legs, coupled with a tingling sensation put me out of work indefinitely. All of those things were building my strength to take on what God had in store for me, which was far better than any corporation could offer.

You're probably thinking, *well, how can losing your job be part of God's plan and being stricken with a lifelong medical condition be a blessing in disguise?* There's a period when God will test your faith, especially in moments of adversity. "And the Lord turned the captivity of Job, when he prayed for his friends: also, the Lord gave Job twice as much as he had before." (Job 42:10, KJV). Job lost everything. God will send tests your way to see how you're going to respond. If you put your faith in Him and do what you're supposed to do, He will bless you with more like He did for Job. When we speak of the word faith, it is when you are able preserve in the midst of a storm. God and Satan made a bet if taking his family and his wealth would make him turn from God. Job surpassed his test of faith by putting his trust in God's hands despite what others were encouraging him to do so as a result God blessed him abundantly.

"After experiencing an adverse event, you will be at a crossroads. You can either view it as a blessing or allow your past to control the rest of your life."

Through research on additional ways to overcome adversity, I stumbled across some interesting tips Tiffany Mason wrote in an article for Psych Central: "Four Proven Ways to Overcome Adversity." I wanted to share them with you to try whenever you feel life is throwing those bricks at you.

1. **Surround yourself with positive people.** Be selective with the people you surround yourself with. Indirectly, they will affect your mood and your outlook. When you are in an emotional state, it's important to surround yourself with people who are supportive and encouraging. Human beings conform to those around them. Conformity is the change of behavior caused by another person or group of people. When experiencing adversity, it's crucial in your development to surround yourself with people who are accepting of your flaws, mistakes, and imperfections.
2. **Write.** There is something so peaceful in writing down your thoughts. However short or long your journal entries are, the process of writing down your emotions allows you to reflect. There are many benefits to writing:
   - Allows for self-expression
   - Helps give feedback about your life
   - Avows you to better understand your current situation
   - Gives you permission to think outside the box

Writing in a journal once a day can help you overcome adversity. Whatever emotions, feelings, or thoughts come to mind, jot them down. Years from now, you'll be able to reflect and see just how much you have developed.

1. **Start investing in yourself.** There is no greater investment than your own personal development. Experiencing adversity is a great excuse for people not to take charge of their lives. We all face adversity in some way. What makes one individual succeed and another not is how they handle their adversity. Many of us allow challenges to defeat us. What we need to focus on is developing into a stronger and wiser individual because of the challenges. There is no better way to do so than developing your internal world.

Your adversity is a blessing in disguise. You may not think so at the moment, but it will eventually make you stronger and wiser. (Mason, 2014)

Adversity has hit many of the rich and famous, and they've been able to turn their tragic incidents into something positive. I would be willing to bet it's not because they're superheroes, but because they've had the ability to look beyond the circumstances using their resilience, strength, and wisdom, all of which we as human beings have the ability to do if we work and trust we can overcome. "Success isn't always easy, and the road to achieving it can be bumpy. Even some of the world's most successful and famous people, including J. K. Rowling, Steve Jobs, and Oprah Winfrey, lost their jobs and overcame challenges before they became someone whose name almost everyone would recognize." The process may look different for every individual due to the nature of the trauma. Let's take a look at a few celebrities and how they weathered the storm in the midst of adversity. (Doyle, 2020)

According to a December 2017 *HuffPost* article "8 Celebrities Who Transformed Tragedy into Something Positive" by Alena Hall, Jennifer Hudson lost her mother, brother, and nephew in a span of three days after William Balfour, her elder sister's estranged husband, brutally shot and killed them in what prosecutors deemed a fit of rage. Despite her unfathomable pain, Hudson not only learned to forgive Balfour, but also created the Julian D. King Gift Foundation in honor of her nephew. The foundation aims to "provide stability, support, and positive experiences for children of all backgrounds to help enable them to grow to be productive, confident, and happy adults." On July 31, 2013, Hudson was honored at the Do Something Awards for her incredible work.

What about Simone Biles, the American gymnast who is considered one of the greatest athletes of all times? In the summer of 2021, she was in the spotlight not only for her athletic abilities, but for dropping out of the Tokyo Olympics. She decided at the last minute not to perform, leaving her team high and dry when they needed her most. The world was upset with her decision. Perhaps the world was more concerned about the glory of taking home the medal than the wellbeing of a human. Simone had been battling mental health issues, so she took a break. "What makes all of Biles' outstanding achievements even more remarkable is the amount of adversity she has had to overcome on her pathway to the top. Biles was born in Columbus, Ohio. She and her three siblings ended up in the foster care system after their mother was unable to care for them. Her ascent to the top of the world of gymnastics began around the same time she was adopted by her maternal grandfather, who raised her just outside of Houston, Texas. Biles first tried the sport as part of a field trip and quickly showed immense potential. She burst onto the national scene in 2012 with a win at the American Classic hosted in Huntsville, Texas, and joined the US Junior National Team later that year." (Thompson, 2021)

The stories shared in this chapter prove we can go on after a bout of adversity. Of course, some conditions were more extreme than others, and every individual process things differently. A mindset shift needs to cultivate when something "bad" happens. You have to be hopeful and open to change and invite positive people into your space. Instead of asking, "Why me," figure out ways to say, "Not me." "When experiencing adversity, it's crucial in your development to surround yourself with people who are accepting of your flaws, mistakes, and imperfections. Overcoming adversity can be a challenge; when you have a supportive team helping you move forward, it's much easier to accept yourself." (Mason, 2014).

UNDERSTANDING POST-TRAUMATIC GROWTH
Let's work on bouncing back and growing through the circumstances. There is such thing as post-traumatic growth (PTG). "The phenomenon was identified by psychologists Richard Tedeschi and Lawrence Calhoun in the 1990s. Based on their research, the pair described five categories of growth that occur over time: Survivors of trauma recognize and embrace new opportunities. They forge stronger relationships with loved ones as well as with victims who suffered

in the same way. They cultivate inner strength through the knowledge they have overcome tremendous hardship. They gain a deeper appreciation for life. And their relationship to religion and spirituality changes and evolves." (Psychology Today staff, 2021)

CULTIVATING GROWTH AFTER TRAUMA
"Trauma survivors who want to cultivate growth can strive to process the experience once they have space from it. It's nearly impossible to evolve in the middle of a crisis, but reflection in its aftermath can provide a foundation for growth. Survivors can explore how the experience changed their mindset, if they appreciate life in a new way, whether their relationships have deepened, or whether they embody a new sense of spirituality." (Psychology Today staff, 2021)

Everything isn't what it seems; you can hide behind the hurt, but it will come out. In the end, the choice is yours. Do you want to lay down from that blow or get up, fight, and be the best version of yourself? Adversity is here to grow you, like fertilizer to plants.

REFLECTIONS:

PAIN TO POWER PLAN
Transformation starts with you.

EMOTIONAL:

What are some ways you can change your feelings toward adversity, taking your thoughts from "it's over" to "I'm living"?

PHYSICAL:

We know adversity can happen at any time. What can you do more of when it comes your way?

MENTAL:

What are ways you can shift your mindset to cultivate growth?

PAIN TO POWER PLAN

Transformation starts with you!

Emotional

Physical

Mental

CHAPTER 7

ABANDONMENT

"To anyone out there who's hurting—it's not a sign of weakness to ask for help. It's a sign of strength."

BARACK OBAMA

Kim is a forty-eight-year-old retail manager. In her spare time, she loves playing with makeup and making women feel beautiful by caring for their skin as a Mary Kay consultant. Kim is happily married with three children and loves spending time with her family, especially her grandson. They spend lots of time together on her days off, doing everything her grandson loves. She takes him to his favorite eating spots, and they even do rounds on his go-kart. Kim had the perfect life, happily married with a beautiful family. Then unexpectedly, the happiness came crashing down and hit her like a ton of bricks.

Kim received the news of her youngest sibling's passing due to her long battle with drug addiction. Death is never easy, but it's even harder when it's unexpected. Then to throw salt on the fresh wound, her mother was fighting a heavy battle no one knew about. She gave in to her silent struggle and took her life the following year in 2017. "The grief process is always difficult, but a loss through suicide is like no other, and the grieving can be especially complex and traumatic. People coping with this kind of loss often need more support than others but may get less. There are various explanations for this. Suicide is a difficult subject to contemplate. Survivors may be reluctant to confide the death was self-inflicted. And when others know the circumstances of the death, they may feel uncertain about how to offer help. Grief after suicide is different, but there are many resources for survivors and many ways you can help the bereaved." (Harvard Health Publishing, 2019)

As Kim and I talked through her devastation, she shared her opinion of trauma and grief. Could you imagine the devastation Kim experienced within one year? Kim is the oldest of three and she has a surviving sibling who lives thousands of miles away, so she endured the pain of losing two loved ones and the fear of what's next alone. A loved one's suicide is a very deep wound, and to think your loved one was fighting a battle you had no control over and everyone missed it—it was a dark secret to the world.

Do you know trauma and stigma can accompany suicide deaths? "The recent, untimely deaths of Kate Spade, reportedly from depression-related suicide, and of Anthony Bourdain, also from apparent suicide, came as a surprise to many. How could a fashion designer and businesswoman known for her whimsical creations and a chef, author, and television personality who embodied a lust for life be depressed enough to end their lives? Crushing sadness can hide behind many facades. According to a report by the US Centers for Disease

Control and Prevention (CDC), suicide rates for adults in the United States are on the rise. Since 1999, suicide rates in twenty-five states increased by over 30 percent. In the US, suicide accounted for nearly forty-five thousand deaths in 2016. Each person who dies by suicide leaves behind an estimated six or more "suicide survivors"—people who've lost someone they care about deeply and are left grieving and struggling to understand." (CDC, 2020)

Do you think people are more compassionate when someone dies by suicide today than in years past? Kim, experiencing this firsthand, shared with me her thoughts on people who commit suicide. Her original perception before she went through it was, in her words, they were selfish and attention seekers. She learned the stigmas were false and totally changed her perspective on her thoughts of suicide. How many times do we encounter people who don't really understand your pain until they've actually experienced it for themselves? Never allow anyone to dictate your level of pain or your traumatic experience. It's yours, not theirs.

As you can imagine, Kim was in a really dark place for two years, harboring the resentment, abandonment, anger, guilt, and other emotions that came with a traumatic event. She started trying to piece her life back together, so she eventually sought out professional counseling, getting paired with a psychiatrist. At that time, she was placed on heavy medications to calm the demons she was fighting.

Kim said, "Most days, I felt like a walking zombie and had no desire to lead a life in that way." At that point, Kim recalled saying, "They wouldn't want me to live my life like this." She had to come up with a coping skill of her own. She also wanted to feel like herself again.

She went cold turkey, gave up the medication, and started focusing on loving herself more. Can you imagine the crushing guilt and grief a loved one deals with long after the loss of a suicide victim? A lot of times, family members who experience the suicide of a loved one will begin to blame or question themselves, wondering if they could've done anything to prevent it from happening. The surviving family members potentially go through fear, disbelief, and shame to name a few other emotions. If you're wondering if Kim embraced these emotions from false beliefs, the answer is "yes"! In fact, she began questioning her role as a sister and a daughter. Kim shared the guilt of wondering, *What if I had intervened? Could I have saved my sister by sending her to a drug rehabilitation center? Did my mother try to show me any warning signs? Did I miss the clues she was planning to take her life?*

Could there be subtle signs of depression we could monitor with our loved ones? It doesn't necessarily mean an individual is planning to take their life if they're experiencing mental health concerns; however, we could get a better understanding of how they're feeling if we knew the warning signs. Truth be told, the perpetrator may not even realize they are depressed. "Symptoms of depression can affect a person physically, mentally, and emotionally. Common symptoms include trouble sleeping, appetite changes, and problems concentrating. They affect how you think, what you do, and how you feel physically. A depressed person may not feel motivated to do their usual activities. A person may feel low on energy, lack interest in activities they once enjoyed, or want to isolate themselves from others. Relationships with family members, friends, and coworkers may be affected." (Brown, 2020) Keep in mind depression isn't a one-size-fits-all. It can be triggered by numerous things and can happen to anyone.

Kim would often battle with these thoughts as she went through this heart-wrenching experience. Kim asked herself, "Could I have changed the outcome if I did just a little bit more?" While the pain was still raw and there were still no answers as to why, Kim recalls feeling this was killing her literally. We tend to blame ourselves for others' actions when in actuality, there's nothing we can do when a person has their mind made up. "A close friend of one of my colleagues took her life. It happened as so many suicides do—out of the blue. A few days earlier, my colleague had spent the day hanging out with her friend, who was relaxed, upbeat, and normal. Sadly, suicide without warning is not uncommon. Many people who die by suicide do so without letting on they are thinking about it or planning it, says Dr. Michael Miller, assistant professor of psychiatry at Harvard Medical School." (Skerrett, 2012).

It was then she realized the emotional trauma was taking a toll on her mentally and physically. She finally stopped trying to figure it out and mustered up enough strength to stop questioning things that were out of her control. She would often talk to God. She started thinking about her responsibilities with her three children and her grandson and didn't want them to ever go through what she was living through.

> "Trust in the Lord with all your heart, and do no lean on your own understanding. In all your ways acknowledge Him, and He will make straight paths."
>
> (PROVERBS 3:5 ESV)

When you're dealing with trauma, whether it be physiological or physical, there are a lot of similarities in the associated emotions. During interview sessions, one of the most common themes I noticed was taking blame regardless of the traumatic event. Anyone who's suffered should be assured you have the courage, strength, and vulnerability to transform, resurrect, and reclaim yourself. It's not your fault, but it is your fate (Firestone, 2018). It leads me to ask, "Is this real or a false belief due to the psychological elements?" The best way to embrace issues that show up is to process that with a therapist. That is both inward and outward, so you get deep to the root cause to help you maneuver through life in a more positive light and realize the world doesn't stop because of something out of your control.

In the beginning, Kim was very unhappy and angry she wasn't able to prevent either of the situations; however, she felt they had their minds made up. She finally understood there was nothing anyone could've done to prevent the tragic events. Instead, she held onto the great memories of both her sister and mother. Kim would have flashbacks often and recount her relationship with her mother, slowly coming to terms with going from talking to her mother every single day to not being able to talk to her at all.

As time went on, Kim realized her sister and mother made a choice and they didn't want her opinion in the choices they made, so therefore, ultimately, she had no impact on the outcome. As with any traumatic situation, there is a process. Kim said it took her some time to get there, but the consequences of their actions were beyond her control.

When I asked Kim how she copes with the situation on a day-to-day basis, Kim stated, "I want to share my biggest piece of advice: Please understand it is okay and normal to grieve, and there will be triggers. Don't drown in the situation; don't allow the emotions to consume you. Do things that make you happy. If it's shopping, go shopping. The things that make you happy may be what play a major role in your healing process. Treat the situation as temporary and know it will resurface. Just be prepared to deal with the emotions head on so you're not stuck." To this day she still deals with the darkness; however, she's found ways to move forward.

Kim also shared a recent experience from her business. She was challenged with an incentive during May—Mental Health Awareness Month—that hit home really hard. The incentive was to have a discussion on suicide prevention. Just imagine sitting in a meeting of strangers with no one knowing your personal trauma and to having that hit you in the gut. It was no one's fault she took this really hard and had to excuse herself from the meeting.

As we know, triggers will hit us intentionally or unintentionally. In this case, it was unintentional. Kim had to regroup before returning to the meeting after explaining to her director the reason for her emotions. Once she explained, the group was very supportive and respectful. Sometimes, when you've experienced trauma, you think everyone is or should be aware of your feelings. There will be situations where, as in this case, no one knows, so the trigger is unpreventable. You have to learn ways to navigate without allowing the trauma to dictate your life.

Kim said, "Never allow others to tell you how to grieve or work through your trauma. Remember, these are your emotions, and no one can tell you how you should feel or how fast you should move on. Everyone grieves and deals with trauma differently, so if it takes you longer than other people, know it's normal. There will be spurts, good days and bad days; don't allow anyone to tell you how to get through your process or that you should be over the pain, except if you have access to a mental health professional."

If you're a friend or family of the person going through the traumatic experience, be mindful of your words, even if it's with great intentions, because there is no manual on how to cope with the loss of a loved one. If you're not comfortable, just be a listening ear. In some cases, you may unintentionally say the wrong thing that causes more harm than good.

To keep her mother and sister close in her heart, Kim has pictures of them both all over her house, office, and desk at work. This is her reminder of the great people who were in her life, and she will never forget about them. Kim also wants other people to know, and when they visit the office or her home, they can ask about those pictures and she can remember all the good times. She wants her grandson to always remember his great-grandmother and great-aunt. She often tells him funny stories of what her mother would do when she was growing up as a young kid to show him how wonderful his great-grandmother.

Don't beat yourself up; get the help you need so you can find ways to move forward. Kim shared while the pain still exists, she is in a place now where she is considering of donating her time to a suicide hotline as a consultant in another year. The hotline would be dedicated in her mother's honor as a support to bring awareness and a listening ear. She would be able to share her experience with families who are going through what she is living through. What an awesome way to give back to all the broken hearts.

"Stigma, shame, and isolation. Suicide can isolate survivors from their community and even other family members. There's still a powerful stigma attached to mental illness (a factor in most suicides) and many religions specifically condemn the act as a sin, so survivors may understandably be reluctant to acknowledge or disclose the circumstances of such a death. Family differences over how to publicly discuss the death can make it difficult even for survivors who want to speak openly to feel comfortable doing so. The decision to keep the suicide a secret from outsiders, children, or selected relatives can lead to isolation, confusion, and shame that may last for years or even generations. In addition, if relatives blame one another—thinking perhaps particular actions or a failure to act may have contributed to events—that can greatly undermine a family's ability to provide mutual support." (*Harvard Women's Health Watch, 2019*)

Remember, if you or a loved one has gone through trauma from suicide, you're probably still dealing with the effects.

The details of the incident and thoughts of how the individual was feeling when they took their own life constantly play over in your mind. It is a perfect time to get in touch with a support group and remembering you're not alone.

SUPPORT FROM OTHER SURVIVORS
"There are many general grief support groups, but those focused on suicide appear to be much more valuable. Some people also find it helpful to be in a group with a similar kinship relationship, so parents are talking to other parents. Some support groups are facilitated by mental health professionals; others by laypersons. If you go and feel comfortable and safe—feel you can open up and won't be judged—that's probably more important than whether the group is led by a professional or a layperson. Layleaders of support groups are often themselves suicide survivors; many are trained by the American Foundation for Suicide Prevention."

Support groups are essential for any type of trauma situation. It gives you an opportunity to feel you're not alone and other individuals are present during the meetings who have gone through similar situations and are able relatable. "For those who don't have access to a group or feel uncomfortable meeting in person, internet support groups are a growing resource. You can join a support group at any time: soon after the death, when you feel ready to be social, or even long after the suicide if you feel you could use support, perhaps around a holiday or an anniversary of the death." (*Harvard Women's Health Watch*, 2020)

A FRIEND IN NEED

"Knowing what to say or how to help after a death is always difficult, but don't let fear of saying or doing the wrong thing prevent you from reaching out to suicide survivors. Don't hold back. Just as you would after any other death, express your concern, pitch in with practical tasks, and listen to whatever the person wants to tell you. Here are some special considerations:

1. "Stay close. Families often feel stigmatized and cut off after a suicide. If you avoid contact because you don't know what to say or do, family members may feel blamed and isolated. Whatever your doubts, make contact. Survivors learn to forgive awkward behaviors or clumsy statements as long as your support and compassion are evident.
2. "Avoid hollow reassurance. It's not comforting to hear well-meant assurances "things will get better" or "at least he's no longer suffering." Instead, the bereaved may feel you don't want to acknowledge or hear them express their pain and grief.
3. "Don't ask for an explanation. Survivors often feel as though they're being grilled: Was there a note? Did you suspect anything? The survivor may be searching for answers, but your role for the foreseeable future is simply to be supportive and listen to what they have to say about the person, the death, and their feelings.
4. "Remember his or her life. Suicide isn't the most important thing about the person who died. Share memories and stories; use the person's name ("Remember when Brian taught my daughter how to ride a two-wheeler?"). If suicide has come at the end of a long struggle with mental or physical illness, be aware the family may want to

recognize the ongoing illness as the true cause of death." (Harvard Medical School, 2019)

With any type of trauma, we never really get over it; we learn ways to move forward, so be kind and respectful of the survivor, much like what Kim shared in her personal story. "Check in on the survivor periodically, and no matter how much you want to help, always be a listening ear." It's easy to say the wrong thing at the wrong time.

We are all in this together. While a suicide can go undetected, it's best to keep your eyes and ears to the ground. If you notice any changes in a friend or family member, don't be afraid to show them you care. Ask, "Is everything okay?" They may not tell you, but you've put them on notice. Be willing to really listen to the individual, because a lot of times, we are so quick to respond.

"Suicide is a leading cause of death in the US. Suicide rates increased in nearly every state from 1999 through 2016. Mental health conditions are often seen as the cause of suicide, but suicide is rarely caused by any single factor. In fact, many people who die by suicide are not known to have a diagnosed mental health condition at the time of death. Other problems often contribute to suicide, such as those related to relationships, substance use, physical health, and job, money, legal, or housing stress." (CDC, 2021)

If you think a loved one or friend might hurt himself or herself, call the National Suicide Prevention Lifeline at 800-273-8255. "We can all help prevent suicide. The Lifeline provides twenty-four hours a day, seven days a week free and confidential support for people in distress, prevention and crisis resources for you or your loved ones, and best practices for professionals." (National Suicide Lifeline Prevention, 2021)

Please make a note that in the summer of 2022 the National Suicide Prevention Lifeline will be "switching to an easy-to-remember **988** for suicide prevention and mental health crisis services will make it easier for Americans in crisis to access the help they need and decrease the stigma surrounding suicide and mental health issues." (FCC, 2021)

"Place your hand over your heart. Can you feel it? That is called purpose. You're alive for a reason, so don't ever give up."
MENTAL HEALTH DAILY, 2021

REFLECTIONS

PAIN TO POWER PLAN
Transformation starts with you.

EMOTIONAL:
If you were grieving from the loss of a loved one, what are some steps you could take to move forward in life? Keep in mind, the loss will forever be in your mind. Let's jot down ways you could move forward.

PHYSICAL:
If you have a loved one who has experienced a loss of a family member through natural causes, you can attest it's not

easy. When an individual has gone through death by suicide, they're left with a lot of unanswered questions. How could you help your friend or family member get through their situations?

MENTAL:
What are some ways you could forgive yourself for something you had no control over?

PAIN TO POWER PLAN
Transformation starts with you!

- Emotional
- Physical
- Mental

CHAPTER 8

THE POWER OF A POSITIVE THOUGHT

"Change your thoughts and you change your world."
                                        NORMAN VINCENT PEALE

Do you ever tell yourself negative things and then wonder why you continue on a negative pattern? Do you think the worse of everything? Do you say bad things about yourself? If you've answered "yes" to any of these questions, you are not alone. We've all been a victim of negative self-talk at some point in our lives for different reasons. In fact, researchers estimate we think about fifty to seventy thousand thoughts a day, and about 80 percent of those thoughts are negative. Whoa, that is a lot of negative self-talk. (Canfield, 2021) When we're constantly thinking negatively, it doesn't allow us to move forward in life. A negative thought diminishes our abilities to actually believe in our full potential. We're always going to find ourselves limiting our abilities by lack of confidence and self-sabotage.

In my personal observations, negative thinking can result from a lack of self-confidence, low self-esteem, and an array of other unhealthy habits that can have a lasting impact on your overall wellbeing. You are a direct reflection of your thoughts and in total control of your thinking. When things don't go as we planned, we tend to automatically think the worse of that situation when in actuality, it requires a simple adjustment that will drastically shift to a positive outcome. If we get in our own headspace, we can talk ourselves out of what we deserve; this becomes self-sabotage without realizing it. If you think you're a failure, you more than likely will be a failure because you're not going to do anything that will make you a success. That's all part of the negative thinking, and your brain is storing those thoughts.

In order to lead healthier and happier lives, we must shift our mindsets. The way we think has a major impact on our everyday actions. If we could optimists instead of pessimists, we would learn being positive is so much more powerful than being negative. It will help you create and transform energy with a mindset to seek healthier and happier results regardless of the circumstances. Yes, bad things can still happen, but so will good things because that's how life works. We don't have to get trapped in those circumstances by our way of thinking. There is so much pleasure in positive thinking, it will transform your life. It starts in your dialogue.

Are you known by your friends as the person who is always beating yourself up with your critical thoughts and talking yourself out of what could be your **purpose** in life? You're not alone; we all have done it at some time or another. I would like to share some research to get you started on transforming your thoughts from an article Amy Morin wrote in a 2018 *INC.* article:

1. Recognize Your Negative Thoughts

"When you get an email from the boss that says, 'I need to meet with you as soon as possible,' is your first thought you're about to be fired or do you think you must be getting a raise?" Oh, my goodness, I have been guilty of this so many times; I automatically think the worst.

2. Look for Evidence Your Thought Is True

"Just because you think something doesn't make it true. In fact, most of your thoughts are more likely to be opinions rather than facts." This is a is a sure sign of a traumatic experience. They are false beliefs because it happened once, so you automatically assume it's going to happen again without knowing all the facts. For example, if you were in a car accident, every time you look in your rear-view mirror and see a car the proper distance behind you, you automatically assume that car is going to rear-end you.

I am here to shed light on thinking positive from a personal perspective. It all starts and ends with you, your brain, and the way you think. Your brain is a muscle that listens to everything you tell it, so why not fuel it with good stuff? It's easier said than done for some people, especially since you've trained that muscle to operate negatively for such a long period.

I'd like to share with you a few positive thinking techniques from my toolkit. I love to start my day with prayer and immediately follow up by speaking positive affirmations to myself.

Are you wondering what a positive affirmation is and why it's beneficial? According to a 2021 *Positive Psychology* article by psychologist Catherine Moore, MBA, positive affirmations are almost as easy to define as they are to practice. Put simply, they are positive phrases or statements used to challenge negative or unhelpful thoughts. Practicing positive affirmations can be extremely simple; all you need to do is pick a phrase and repeat it to yourself. You may choose to use positive affirmations to motivate yourself, encourage positive changes in your life, or boost your self-esteem.

IS THERE SCIENCE BEHIND THEM?
There is a science to positive affirmations. The more you practice, the more you get it. We as humans love reassurance, so what better way to build your own confidence than through affirmations? "Science, yes. Magic, no. Positive affirmations require regular practice if you want to make lasting, long-term changes to the ways you think and feel. The good news is the practice and popularity of positive affirmations are based on widely accepted and well-established psychological theory." (Moore, 2021) I agree with Moore; there is no magic to making yourself overcome negative thoughts. It's a matter of saying nice things to yourself daily.

The next time you start your day, try looking straight into your mirror and saying, "I **am** beautiful. I **am** confident." God reminds us we are everything He says we are, but we must be believers. Trust me, the more you practice, the better you will get. I know that will probably sound a little strange the first time, but it is very powerful. I ask that you embrace the moment because that's all it takes to get your happy juices flowing and is the best way to start your day.

I challenge you—before you head out the door each day, look into your mirror directly and say all of the most positive things you can think of about you. Remember, no one is perfect, but we all have something great we should remind ourselves of each day. Most importantly, you're setting the tone for your entire day. Why not set it off in a positive light? Nothing and no one will be able to disrupt your positive thinking.

Here are more examples you can use to get started:

- I **am** great at what I do
- I **am** courageous
- I **am** a warrior
- I **am** in charge of my own happiness
- I **will** do my best every day to be better than the day before
- I **am** grateful everyday
- I **am** a conqueror

Did you just feel the energy in those affirmations? Did you feel powerful when you listened to how you were fueling your brain with good stuff? Now, do it a little more each day and you can overcome the negative thoughts.

I just shared with you two of the most powerful words in the dictionary to describe myself; now, I would love for you to try this in your spare time using words that best describe you. If you're fully committed to changing the way you think and speak to yourself, I highly recommend you embrace this exercise with an open mind. Be patient, it will take more than one night to identify the transition in the way you feel. But don't worry, if you practice, you'll get it.

Your mindset plays a major part in your day-to-day activities and can impact your thought process. If you're constantly talking negatively, you will be less motivated. Don't tell yourself, "I can't go for this walk because I'm afraid it's going to hurt my back really bad." With that mindset, you're less likely to go for a small walk that could do your body some good.

If we rethink the sentence and say, "You know what, I am going to try to take a small walk today to get some fresh air and exercise because the doctor approves," you're likely to be more motivated because you're looking forward to the good instead of focusing on the problem. I shared that example with you because I found it was holding me back. I was creating fear and unintentionally thinking negatively. "You already know exercise is good for your body, but did you know it can also boost your mood, improve your sleep, and help you deal with depression, anxiety, stress, and more? I found the exercise was so refreshing to leave from inside of the four walls. Instead of allowing your mind to wander, pay close attention to the physical sensations in your joints, muscles, and even your insides as your body moves. Exercises that involve cross movement and engage both arms and legs—such as walking (especially in sand), running, swimming, weight training, or dancing—are some of your best choices." (Robinson, Segal, Smith, 2021)

What's even worse is negative self-talk can be so toxic it can bring on health problems. "It plays a role in prolonging our stress response, and when stress remains chronically elevated over time, it exerts wear and tear on the body. That can result in negative conditions like sleep problems, cardiovascular disease, and even certain cancers." (O'Brien, 2021) I'm certain we all know people like this, but we don't realize the way they think could be the contributing factor to their health issues.

Your thought process is altered and has you believing you're worthless. The more you say and think these things, the more they become reality to you. This, in turn, creates problems in marriages, the workplace, and friendships. No one wants to hang out with a Negative Nancy or Debbie Downer because they spoil all the fun for the optimist.

"Why is transforming your self-talk into a soundtrack of positivity important to your weight loss goals? Because negative self-talk can drive you to overeat as a way to calm or numb yourself. What's more, the physical stress created by negative thoughts can create the metabolic state that makes weight loss difficult, if not impossible. Here are four common types of negative self-talk to watch out for:

- "**Perfectionism/Polarizing:** Things are either good or bad—there's no middle ground. If you're not perfect, you're a total failure.
- "**Catastrophizing:** You dream up the worst possible outcome, and small issues are harbingers of doom.
- "**Rationalization:** You blame yourself for everything bad that happens. For instance, if a few friends don't make it to your party, you assume no one likes you.

- "**Filtering:** You search for the negative aspects of any given situation, filtering out any positive ones. The vacation was mostly great, but you complain to yourself and others about the delayed flight home rather than sharing the delights of the trip.

Negative self-talk can contribute to stress and even depression, which put the body into terrible metabolic state." (Jamieson, 2015)

Here are four ways to help you decrease negative self-talk. While trying these tips, keep in mind that one size doesn't fit all, but it is a general idea to get you started.

IDENTIFY THE TRIGGER

Focus. Evaluate the thought. Ask yourself, *where is this coming from? Is it **fear**?*

"What is the root cause of your negative thoughts? If you don't know where they come from, you can't curb them. You may end up continually exposing yourself to triggers for negative thoughts without bracing yourself in advance, even when it's unnecessary for you to be putting yourself into those situations in the first place. Anxiety can often fill your head with negativity, and you may even convince yourself all your fears will come true." (Butler, 2020)

SHIFT YOUR PERSPECTIVE

Don't think too far in the future; focus on the present. This causes stress and limited beliefs. You can't always look at the big picture. Sometimes it's best to ask yourself, *does this even matter? Will it matter this time next year?*

"Thinking about the future is important for planning purposes, but overly focusing on what is to come will do you no good. After all, though you can prepare and make goals for it, you cannot definitively know what is going to happen in the future. Similarly, thinking about the past is important for self-reflection, which has positive effects on one's sense of self and mental state. But focusing too much on the past is pointless, as you can't change what's happened before." Live in the present. If we think too much on the future, we leave room for disappointments, thinking what is going to come that may never happen (Butler, 2020).

ANTICIPATE GREAT THINGS
Don't always think the worse is going to happen. Be intentional and acknowledge the positive.

"Positive thinking doesn't mean you keep your head in the sand and ignore life's less pleasant situations. Positive thinking just means you approach unpleasantness in a more positive and productive way. You think the best is going to happen, not the worst." (Mayo Clinic Staff, 2021)

Take back your life by breaking free of the negative self-talk. It may seem impossible since you've been doing it for so long, but with your due diligence, it'll be like a soundproof mind. Yes, because you have total control of your thoughts, block the critic inside your head and start viewing from a positive lens. When you see things in a positive light, it doesn't mean your world is going to be without incident. What it means is you're able to process that one-off from the mind of an optimist.

"The inner speech, your thoughts, can cause you to be rich or poor, loved or unloved, happy or unhappy, attractive or unattractive, powerful or weak. Overcoming insecurity begins with your self-thoughts. If you have negative self-thoughts and self-talk, you will feel poor, unloved, unhappy, unattractive, and weak. On the other hand, positive self-talk will help you feel rich in spirit, loved, happy, attractive, and powerful."

RALPH CHARELL (ECONOMY, 2019)

REFLECTIONS:

PAIN TO POWER PLAN
Transformation starts with you.

EMOTIONAL:
How can you control self-talk when you think the worst is going to happen?

PHYSICAL:
How can you be more self-confident in the way you think?

MENTAL:
How can you change my beliefs about negative things?

PAIN TO POWER PLAN

Transformation starts with you!

Emotional

Physical

Mental

CHAPTER 9

HAPPINESS IS AN INSIDE JOB

"Happiness is the new rich. Inner peace is the new success. Health is the new wealth. Kindness is the new cool."

SYED BALKHI

The pursuit of happiness is a real thing, and you can choose to **be happy**. **"Happiness is an inside job; don't assign anyone that much power over your life"** (Hale, 2021). Most people will be surprised at how little control outside influences have over your happiness. When we speak of happiness being an inside job, "you've probably heard that before. But what exactly does it mean? And why is it so hard sometimes to find (and hold onto) your happiness? If you feel like negative events tend to have a big effect on you, or like your emotional state is out of your control, you're definitely not alone. Studies have shown happiness really is an inside job—you just need the right tools." (Hugo, 2021).

Happiness isn't connected to people, places, or things. As we know, outside influences are things we have no control over. People are fickle, the entire world changed abruptly in 2020 by being plagued with a pandemic, and we had absolutely no control to change the circumstances. If you think about it, when we achieve that dream job, new relationship, or new home, life can still happen and cause us to lose all happiness because we were connected to material things that give temporary satisfaction.

"As it turns out, happiness depends on a number of different factors—but some of them are more important than others. Your DNA and personality contribute some, but external factors like popularity or money make up less than you might think. In fact, **you have a lot more control over your happiness than you may believe**. By practicing things like mental resilience, meditation, and gratitude, you can learn to build your happiness from the inside out." (Hugo, 2021)

"Do you ever wonder why you don't seem to feel as happy as the person next to you? Do you ever feel you are on the sidelines looking in on a party you were never invited to? Maybe you seemingly have everything you could possibly want materialistically but still can't quite feel that elusive internal contentment?" (Lum, 2021)

Let's face it—when we have all those things, we're never satisfied; we want more. The newness wears off and the gratification that led us to wanting them in the first place no longer exists. It's like a temporary fulfillment. To those who think it's impossible to choose your happiness internally, let me tell you, it's 100 percent mindset. According to a 2008 study by

Katherine G. Denny and Hans Steiner, who examined elite college-level athletes, they found internal factors (like mindfulness and self-esteem) influenced happiness significantly more than external ones (like performance in school or on the field). We do have control to make ourselves happy. We tend to focus on problems so much we lose sight of happiness. If we place more focus on the fact, we deserve to be happy, we then will not allow anything to dictate otherwise.

I challenge you to embrace a positive mindset, express gratitude, and extend a little grace to yourselves, then nothing will be able to disturb your internal happiness even after multiple attempts.

Want to feel happier? Give yourself a boost by creating a happy life you deserve. In my previous years, it wasn't something I focused on until I had the opportunity to identify what was most important to me. This was after life experiences. I love doing things that make me happy and set my soul on fire. I want to pause here to share some of the simplest, actionable ways I've used. As you review what I've shared below, I must be fully transparent—I am not perfect, I am still a work in progress. However, I am more intentional with my actions, so as a result, I am getting better each day at protecting my happiness. It definitely keeps my happy juices flowing and overall wellbeing intact.

GRATITUDE
Practicing gratitude has a lot to do with our happiness, being able to express happiness with the things we currently have more so than things we would like to have. Think about it,

haven't you worked so hard for something, but it still wasn't enough because you wanted more? We always seem to want more after we get what we thought we wanted. We're never satisfied. It's true what I used to hear growing up as a kid—the more we get, the more we want. As our gratitude practice becomes more sensitive by focusing on what's good in our life along with all of the blessings surrounding us, a certain magic begins to take hold. It's as if we send a message out to the universe to say, "More of this please," which then causes the positive experiences in our life to flourish and grow.

As you flex and work your gratitude muscle every day, it gets stronger. As it develops, so does the realization that it's possible to have a choice about how we respond to the challenges and hurdles life presents us—without getting sucked into a complaining mindset or feeling anxious about what we don't have. As a result, gratitude will impact and transform your life in so many ways:

- Contentment becomes stronger than dissatisfaction
- Peace becomes stronger than frustration
- Appreciation becomes stronger than criticism and complaining
- Resilience to life's challenges increases

Overall, life just becomes sweeter and more fun through practicing gratitude. The happier and more contented we are, the kinder we become to those around us—meaning all who come into contact with us begin to feel the benefits too." (Robertson, 2021)

"If you look to others for fulfillment, you will never truly be fulfilled. If your happiness depends on money, you will never be happy with yourself. Be content with what you have; rejoice in the way things are. When you realize there is nothing lacking, the whole world belongs to you."

LAO TZU (TZU, 2018)

STOP LETTING OTHER PEOPLE GET YOU DOWN (PROJECTION)

We can't worry about what others think of us—that is a sure way to drown your happiness. In most cases, when people are rude, they don't like themselves, so they have to project their insecurities on another person. When you succumb to the drama, you've given them control over you. "Maybe you have a sister who is secretly jealous of you, so she tries to bring you down with little cuts or insults. You have a friend who tells you you're a bad friend. So much of people's meanness is actually a mirror for their own self-esteem issues. The people who tell you that you dress inappropriately are probably the ones who worry about their own looks. The people who accuse us of being dramatic are the ones who bring drama. Don't let projection fool you—see it for what it is, and bless the person on your way out." (Gandhi, 2021)

PRACTICE MINDFULNESS

We know no one's schedule is as flexible these days; some have more time than others. However, you can be mindful and take at least a ten- to fifteen-minute break for yourself each day. Focus on one thing at a time. Take time to pray daily. Meditate as often as you like for at least fifteen minutes.

If you're going to try meditation, there are all sorts of apps for guided meditation for beginners you can research, such as YouTube, Calm, and Headspace. To get started, all you need is a quiet space. Here's what the experts are saying about why mindfulness is beneficial for our overall health:

"Mindfulness is good for our bodies. A seminal study found, after just eight weeks of training, practicing mindfulness meditation boosts our immune system's ability to fight off illness. Practicing mindfulness may also improve sleep quality. Mindfulness is good for our minds: several studies have found mindfulness increases positive emotions while reducing negative emotions and stress. Indeed, at least one study suggests it may be as good as antidepressants in fighting depression and preventing relapse." (*Greater Good*, 2021)

TAKE PICTURES

I love taking lots of pictures of myself, my family, and our favorite furry friend, Lexi. Can you believe an individual had the audacity to inquire as to why I was always taking so many pictures of myself? That was the funniest thing ever to me, for someone to be concerned with the number of pictures I take with my camera. My question was, "Why don't they take pictures?" Guess what? There will be one day when those pictures will be all you have left, so capture all the good times possible.

True happiness is a state of mind that will connect you with your inner you. Learn to be alone. There is so much power in being alone; it gives you the opportunity to enjoy you. Wouldn't it be exciting to learn things about yourself you didn't know? You will inspire yourself without outside influence. Sometimes people think they must have companionship because of fear of being alone. That one day when you spent time with yourself, you'll find peace. You will find so much strength that will grow you to new levels.

When you do what makes you happy, it becomes more of an internal feeling, and it's all within reach. Many of us who choose happiness are aware it requires effort on our part and is done so by being intentional about our actions. What does be intentional mean? Before we dive into a few examples, let's get a clear understanding of intention. Being intentional is when you're putting in a conscious effort daily to show up as the absolute best version of yourself. This means you are making choices based on your actions and feelings to align with your happiness. You're not dependent on people, places, or things to dictate your happiness, but instead, you take total control of being happy! This is a learned behavior. You, too, can choose to **be happy** so your entire wellbeing is aligned.

HERE'S THREE STEPS TO BEING INTENTIONAL

1. **Remove Distractions** – A distraction is anything that doesn't allow you to give your full attention. If you're not giving your full attention, that could cause a disruption to your peace and happiness. You have to ask yourself, "What's more important? My inner happiness or pleasing others?" A few examples of distractions could be social media, cell phone usage, gaming, texting, talking, etc.
2. **Choose to Be Kind** – By being kind to yourself and others, you will experience a positive outcome and feel extremely happy. When we practice kindness, either to

other people or ourselves, we can experience positive mental and physical changes through lowering stress levels and increasing the body's production of feel-good hormones such as dopamine, oxytocin, and serotonin. Being kind helps boost the immune system and reduce blood pressure, stress, and anxiety. The great thing is it isn't difficult to be kind (Thornton, 2021). As the Dalai Lama said, "Be kind whenever possible. It is always possible." (Sharpe, 2020)

3. **Avoid Comparison** – When you compare yourself to others, you get distracted from how well you're actually doing. In most cases, when you're looking at others, you start feeling bad about yourself. It's the illusions that are presented that differ from the reality of how they're actually doing. There are always people who look happier and have more than you. "Beware the danger of comparisons. We live in a world of TV, advertising, and social media that constantly show us how we are not yet living the perfect life, how we don't measure up to other people. Don't fall into the comparison trap because this is one route to lots of negative self-talk and critique. The very opposite of kindness, in fact." (Thornton, 2021)

4. **Become a Psychotic Optimist** – Never count yourself out; always count you **in first**. It is about being content with your status. Whether it happens or not, at the end of the day, be happy with yourself. "Psychotic optimism is believing awesomeness will come to you—no matter what. For example, if you're single, you will no longer say, 'I'm too old to find love—who knows if it'll happen.' You replace it with, 'Love will come to me…it's a when, not an if!' And then you act in accordance with that! You keep yourself **up** because you know love will come to you. Even

if you go on twenty bad dates, you stay psychotically optimistic—and that keeps you in the game!" (Gandhi, 2021)

Hopefully you find my tips helpful and considerable. There are so many other ways you can find your own happiness. Once you incorporate what you've learned, you can add them to your toolkit and be intentional each morning before you start your day. It will be so empowering to realize you're the only one responsible for your happiness and all the accompanying benefits rely solely on you.

If you care for yourself on the inside, it will allow you to free up energy to care for others who are counting on you.

Now that you're equipped, don't you dare miss out on the opportunity to care for yourself. Crank the vibrations up spiritually, mentally, and physically on happiness. This is fuel for your mind, body, and soul.

"I've learned no matter what happens, or how bad it seems today, life does go on, and it will be better tomorrow."
MAYA ANGELOU (GOODREADS, 2021)

REFLECTIONS:

PAIN TO POWER PLAN
Transformation starts with you.

EMOTIONAL:

What is a joyful activity you can do more to feel internal happiness?

PHYSICAL:

What type of activities can you do to make you more mindful of your inner self?

MENTAL:

Have you ever compared yourself to someone else? How did it make you feel? What will you do in the present to avoid comparison to others and recognize you are more than enough?

PAIN TO POWER PLAN

Transformation starts with you!

Emotional

Physical

Mental

CHAPTER 10

UNPLUG, RECHARGE, AND RESET

"Almost everything will work again if you unplug it for a few minutes—including you."

ANNE LAMOTT

What if you could give yourself permission to stop and take a break after a tough week with the job, friends, family, and hustle and bustle of life? Do you ever think you deserve a change from the mundane? These questions can only be answered by you and will require you to accept the fact you can't live life on empty. What does it mean to unplug, recharge, and reset? Just how it sounds: stop doing what you're doing currently, give yourself a break right now, and decide whether you will do this new thing as a daily, monthly, or yearly routine. Don't expect it to happen all at once, but I promise, if you try it, you'll want to do it more often. Self-care is necessary, especially after going through a traumatic experience. I didn't realize just how important it was until I was on disability from my job. This time allowed me to get in tune with my inner self and understand why I really needed to show up as my **best** self.

"We know what we *should* do, but various forces and things inside and outside of our control often stand in the way. But we also know when we are practicing self-care well, the benefits overflow into all the areas of our life—for the better!" (Reed, 2021)

"Traumatic events take different forms—natural disasters (earthquakes, tornados, wildfires), personal loss, school shootings, and community violence—and their effects on us vary. People may feel sad, confused, scared, or worried. Others may feel numb or even happy to be alive and safe. Reactions to traumatic events can be had by those directly impacted as well as by friends and family of victims, first responders, and people learning about the events from the news. Feeling stressed before or after a traumatic event is normal. Coping well with stress begins with recognizing how we are reacting and then by taking steps to manage our reactions in a healthy way." (CDC, 2017)

Life throws unexpected blows which come from unexpected traumatic experiences or the headaches of an ever-changing world. In those moments, we easily gaze over the experiences before we realize we're in an unfamiliar territory of feeling we're stuck or burnt out. This is a perfect time to hit the reset button on our lives to show up as our best selves, feeling rejuvenated and refreshed.

Let's think about the battery in a car; at some point, it will need a jump-start if it is constantly running or being overworked without getting the proper juice to operate at full capacity. If this continues, a jump-start will no longer get the car working again; it could require you to replace the entire battery. If we think about us as humans, if we're fortunate, we have the ability to identify when we are running low on energy so we can jump-start mentally and physically by unplugging, recharging, and resetting. When we do this, we are giving ourselves the opportunity to work again and show up as our best selves. When we as individuals require an unplug, recharge, and reset, our bodies need a mental and or physical break. Unlike the battery, though, it's not just that simple—we can't be replaced.

Being very intentional with unplugging is a sure way to recharge, reset, and guarantee everything will work again. Unplug from your day-to-day routine, social media, and the lengthy to-do list and get out of your head for a while. Relax and drink a cup of coffee, tea, or whatever is your favorite beverage.

It's Friday evening and you've had a long week at work. The weekend is here so let's do something out of the ordinary. Take a break from the day to day. Take time out for yourself doing exactly what makes you happy! This can be reading a book, binge-watching your favorite Netflix series, taking a walk in the park, listening to and singing your favorite music playlist, or even creating more music for your playlist. If you're creating a playlist, I recommend you get creative and have a song for whatever you're struggling with in the moment. You'd be surprised how music can pull you out of a dark place. "There are few things that stimulate the brain the way music does," says one Johns Hopkins otolaryngologist.

"If you want to keep your brain engaged throughout the aging process, listening to or playing music is a great tool. It provides a total brain workout. Research has shown listening to music can reduce anxiety, blood pressure, and pain as well as improve sleep quality, mood, mental alertness, and memory." (John Hopkins Medicine, 2021)

What I've shared isn't a one-size-fits-all approach; it is more so hoping you will find what you enjoy best and make the time to do it! It's amazing how you feel after just giving yourself a little bit of time caring for yourself. You will have a ready-for-the-world mentality after unplugging, recharging, and resetting. In order for this to work, you must unplug, recharge, and reset your mind, body, and soul. This includes walking away from social media for a few hours or even a full day, whatever works best for you. For me, it would be based off of my schedule for the day so I could determine where the most breaks are needed. It can get a little overcrowded out there in the social media world with negativity or even just too much technology in one day. "As social media gains influence, we live less in the moment and more in a world full of filters, photoshop, and false realities that affect our mental health and happiness." (Shoaf, 2020)

So many times, people will feel guilty and find it very difficult to shut down and take the necessary time. It seems people feel guilty the most when they have to leave work early for scheduled doctor's appointments. In some cases, people feel guilty when they take "me time" away from their families. Have you ever heard someone say they were feeling guilty because they took the day off, stayed home, and did absolutely nothing?

In order for you to lead a happy life full of energy, these things are necessary, so if you feel you're not able to make the decision to do what's crucial for your wellbeing, grab yourself an accountability partner. Once you've taken the time out that your body is desperately screaming for, it's now time to celebrate yourself for having the courage to unplug, recharge, and reset. Yes, you need the courage because it's not always easy, especially since we're living in a digital world, and everyone feels the need to stay connected. When the work week rolls around, you will be more than ready to take on those extra projects without feeling the effects of a burnout—therefore it's a win-win. You've cared for yourself and now you're handling business so you can continue to do more of the things you love.

How many times have you created a to-do list and found you never completed it in one day? Even more discouraging, you added to the list as the day went by. It became a never-ending list. We all have at some time or another, so that is even the more reason to make time for yourself. It's our responsibility to create the time to unplug, recharge, and reset, because no one will do it for us.

It is very easy to feel you must get everything done in one day. Let's have that same thought process for allowing ourselves a chance to unplug, recharge, and reset. To get that time to step away, you can prioritize the things based off of importance. Do it consciously, and if necessary to hold yourself accountable, set alarms on your cell phone to take breaks and walk away from that laptop. I mention walking away from your laptop because we tend to take lunch at our desk or with our computers in hand. If the weather permits, get outside to take a fresh air break, and enjoy the sounds of nature.

Now is the perfect time for an unplug, recharge, and reset break, so I will share ways I personally love to take breaks.

SEVEN PAIN TO POWER TIPS:

POSITIVE AFFIRMATIONS

It may seem weird the first time around, but make a conscious effort to look in the mirror every morning and remind yourself of whatever you're feeling or may encounter that day—I **am** capable, I **am** deserving of a break, and I **am** confident. If you feel it was a bad day, go home and repeat the mirror trick, but this time, remind yourself you're not a failure, you just had a bad day. "'Positive affirmations are brief phrases which, when repeated frequently, are meant to encourage positive, happy feelings, thoughts, and attitudes and challenge negative or unhelpful thoughts the person is experiencing,' says Dr. Stacey Schell, a registered clinical psychologist. 'For example, if you're thinking about how you're likely going to fail at some tasks, you might use a positive affirmation to challenge those thoughts.'" (Henderson, 2021)

TREAT YOURSELF TO A SPA DAY

While I don't do this as often as I would love to, it's a great way to unplug, recharge, and reset away from the world. This a great opportunity to relax those tense muscles with a hot stone treatment and massage your temples to relieve the tension headache you've been dealing with all week.

GOING TO THE PARK-GET OUT IN NATURE OR AROUND WATER

Tune into nature. Listening to the bird's chirp is one of my favorite "unplug, recharge, and reset" moments. The park I enjoy most has water, but it's not necessary so my visits consist of resting in the car with the seat reclined all the way back in a resting position. If you have time, take your lunch or snacks with you. There will be no distractions and you can stay as long as time permits. The ability to block out the outside noise of the world paired with the sound of the water is a calming peace like no other. This is something you can do year-round as long as you dress appropriately for the season. Take a blanket, snacks, earbuds, and your favorite playlist. If you visit the same park, change up the scenery by parking in a different area on each visit. Breathing fresh air, basking in the sun, and taking in all the different sounds of nature is medicine for the mind.

LIGHT EXERCISE

I have to take it extremely easy when exercising. However, the body still enjoys a little movement and blood flow. If you have the physical ability to do more, do it; your body will thank you! "Find an outdoor workout that fits your style, whether it's rock climbing, hiking, renting a canoe, or just taking a jog in the park. Plus, all that Vitamin D acquired from soaking up the sun (while wearing sunscreen, of course) can lessen the likelihood of experiencing depressive symptoms." (Breene, 2017)

LISTEN TO MOTIVATION SPEECHES

These are especially great to kick-start your week on a Sunday evening or Monday morning. It's even beneficial to listen each day before heading out the door or driving down the highway if you want to start and end your day in happiness. Remember, how you start your day sets the tone for how your day or week will go. Be intentional with your selection to fit where you are in your life at the time. This could be especially helpful to give you that push you need to get you going to your next level. There are several motivational speeches you can find on YouTube, or you can enter "motivational speeches" in the search engine of Google and find a plethora of motivation.

DECLUTTER

Clean your workspace each day and get rid of clutter in your home. Get rid of toxic people in your space. Did you know there are declutter experts? You can literally pay people to come in and help you organize your home. Check this out: "In many ways, decluttering your home is a lot like trying to get in shape. We all know what we need to do—eat less and exercise more—but going it alone can be overwhelming; often it is easier to follow a plan someone else has created, for both the tips and the inspiration it provides. Hold each item in your hands to see if it sparks joy inside you; if not, thank the item for its service and pass it on to someone else who can use it.

"Overwhelmed with too much stuff? This would be giving you a boost to remove things that no longer suit you. While you're at it, this would work with people who no longer bring joy into your space. If any tidying task takes a minute or less to complete, do it as soon as you think of it.

"These little choices add up to positive habits. This idea is perfect if you're looking to boost your spirits (or are prone to whistling while you work)." (Maze, 2020)

Now that you've had the time to unplug, recharge, and reset with my helpful tips and ideas, it is so easy to fall back into the mindset of not unplugging, recharging, and resetting, so let's reflect. Look back and access how you felt when you made the conscious effort to unplug, recharge, and reset. I know you were excited to get back to the grind of things since that is what you're always telling yourself. However, if you're really honest with yourself, you will admit you felt well-rested and accomplished.

Remember car battery was at a place where we could give it a jump-start to get it operating to full capacity. Once the car was back operating at full capacity, it was ready to go until the next time the owner decides to misuse it by draining its juice. That is an unintentional act because no one wants their car to clunk out on them. Now, let's think about you and your internal battery. You've been intentional with your "unplug, restart, and reset" tactics, so as those to-do lists continue to grow, don't forget to put yourself at the top of the list so you make time for yourself. You will be well-rested and fully charged. Remember, there are people counting on you, so in order to be available for them, you must unplug, recharge, and reset.

You're probably thinking to unplug, recharge, and reset for you isn't as simple as changing a car battery. You're right, there is more to it! However, it is necessary, doable, and dependent upon how you want to treat your wellbeing. You have to be willing to put in the effort as you do for your job each day. This time, it's your turn to care for you. This can cause burnout if you don't catch it in time. If it's work that is getting in the way, take a day off—do it; you're worth it! There is no way you can continue to stay powered up if you don't take the time to unplug, recharge, and reset.

If you take the time to slow down and do it often, you will not clunk out like that drained battery. I encourage you to incorporate all of these tips into your life for at least one hour per day. If you do the math, that would be only seven hours of taking care of yourself and giving you that boost your mind and body deserves.

"Your body and mind will tell you what you need to do—your job is to listen to them. Get plenty of rest when you're tired and use the energy you have if you experience hyperactivity at times. Don't force yourself to be active if you don't have the energy; rest when you feel tired. You may need to talk repetitively about the trauma. If you can find someone who is willing to listen, talk to her/him about how you are feeling. If you do not have anyone in your support network to use, consider calling a crisis line, going to a crisis center, or using other community resources—they are there to help you. Don't make any major life decisions or changes if at all possible. This is not a time to put pressure on yourself to do anything out of the ordinary. Concentrate on taking care of yourself. Do things that feel good to you—take baths, read, watch television, fix yourself a special treat, or whatever else feels nurturing and self-caring." (University of Notre Dame, 2021)

All of these things will allow you the headspace to properly care for your storms when they come. Although storms are uncomfortable, you'll feel better equipped because of how you've taken care of your mental space.

Your mind, body and soul will love you for recognizing what was needed to allow you to be more present in your life and less stressful. At the end of the day, take care of **you**—you owe it to **you**!

"Self-care is giving the world the best of you instead of what's left of you."

KATIE REED (2021)

REFLECTIONS:

PAIN TO POWER PLAN
Transformation starts with you.

EMOTIONAL:
The way you start your day sets the tone for the rest. After reading this book, what three affirmations can you start your day with? After a long day, how can you affirm yourself before getting into bed?

PHYSICAL:

What are some ways you can recharge your internal battery daily? How will you hold yourself accountable to ensure you're recharged?

MENTAL:

If you're currently using social media platforms, can you try to take a four-hour break each day to help with your mental space?

PAIN TO POWER PLAN

Transformation starts with you!

Emotional

Physical

Mental

CHAPTER 11

CONCLUSION: DEALING WITH TRAUMA

"Our job is not to deny the story, but to defy the ending—to rise strong, recognize our story, and rumble with the truth until we get to a place where we think, yes. This is what happened. This is my truth. And I will choose how the story ends."

BRENÉ BROWN

It's clear my trauma didn't, hasn't, and will not define me as a human being. As a matter of fact, trauma has taught me vulnerability and how to cope with the shock and aftermath in a unique and valuable way. The best thing I could've done to save myself was create my personal healing journey. In the light of the stories covered here, trauma can be sneaky; we never know the day nor the hour of the hit. It is best to believe it will be an event, a series of events, or a circumstance that can lead to physical or emotional harm causing lasting effects. If you survive such an event, it is your responsibility to save yourself. In the long run, you have the ability to dictate whether you're going to live in the darkness or allow the little lightbulb in your head to come on so you can see how to navigate your life in a positive manner. All characters in this book decided to allow the lightbulb to switch on by developing resilience through prayer, mindset shifts, self-determination, self-love, self-help, and counseling sessions. As a result, we are leading happier lives and showing up as resilient, empowering, strong, confident, and brave women on a mission to share our truths with the world in an effort to save one life at a time.

Given these points, trauma can be overwhelming and result in some of the most painful moments leading to uncontrollable emotions of feeling betrayed, abandoned, embarrassed, depressed, and ashamed—all of which are normal but can be unhealthy if left untreated. Even though only you can decide your level of pain and how long you go through your process, recovery is possible. The excellent news? If it's identified in a timely manner and you're willing to invest in your wellbeing and kick the victim mentality, you can start the process by proactively caring for yourself through mindfulness. It's an investment in your worth.

Although trauma is treatable, you can experience trauma triggers. These triggers can show up at any moment without notice by simple reminders. You could be driving along the highway and see a billboard or a sign that has an image of that thing that caused you trauma. My trigger was anyone mentioning the telecommunications company in my presence. Before my healing journey, I would feel a knot in my throat and a pit in my stomach that reminded me of that day I was fired due to not being able to get my health in order before they expected. Sometimes people who have been in a car accident may avoid a certain route so they don't pass the scene of the tragic accident. An individual may hear a song on the radio that triggers memories of a sour relationship, and they instantly turn off the radio.

In the event you experience trauma triggers, it is important you're proactive with your self-care plan so you're ready to combat them and move forward. By all means, allow those triggers into your space so you can feel them instead of avoiding them. "Why would I want to feel uncomfortable?" you're probably asking. Let me help you. The more you let them in and deal with them, the better you will be at combating them; instead of feeling like you're about to explode, you're able to celebrate your emotional progress.

As much as people believe the world is over when they go through trying times, it is important to know as you're dealing with your trauma, some things can help you compartmentalize your life, so it doesn't spiral out of control due to an unforeseen event. Trauma isn't a death sentence, but by no means is it comfortable either. As long as you have breath to breathe, you can weather the storm just as you have with any of the other trials and tribulations. We all survived our storms.

"You can't have triumph without conflict. If you're going to have triumph, you can't be a winner if you're not in a fight."
                                                                T. D. JAKES (2021)

In case you're wondering, I persevered through the storm by engaging in more of what I loved by shining my positive light over the world using the techniques from this book. What I didn't know at the time was God's plan over my life. That's how I came out of my tragic event, leading to a victorious life. I decided the job loss wasn't going to steal my joy and the disability wasn't going to rule me. I was able to turn my pain into power by creating a business. I authored my first book that serves to help others who go through traumatic experiences. I've already sold several book talks that I will host all across the world and will appear on upcoming podcast shows. You, too, can overcome and succeed when life tries to knock you off your feet.

I was determined not to allow my circumstances to take the best of me. Through my resilience and God, I had the power to push beyond what came to destroy what I had built over the years. I stood on my faith, which reminded me everything happens for a reason. Though we may not understand at the time it's happening, God will surely reveal it in time.

All things considered, if you or someone you know has gone through a traumatic experience, this book is designed to help you see beyond the circumstance by aiding in solving your problems. You will have the ability to live a more fulfilled life instead of getting lost in the trauma. You will find the more you welcome the feelings of your triggers, the more you will be equipped and notice you can apply these techniques to your everyday life. In fact, you will have more peace of mind and serenity. Are you ready to test your resilience? It starts with an open mind and realizing nothing is a one-size-fits-all approach. If necessary, grab a friend or family member or start a support group to jump-start your healing journey by implementing what you've learned in this book. My prayer is you are able to see the light and understand there is **hope** in your struggle. Lastly, you get to choose how your story ends, so go ahead, activate your faith, trust the process, and treat yourself by taking the first step to creating the best version of yourself.

REFLECTIONS:

PAIN TO POWER PLAN
Transformation starts with you.

EMOTIONAL:
After reading through the chapters, have you identified ways to feel your emotions that are caused by your trauma triggers? If so, what is one thing you're going to do differently when those feelings come to ensure you're progressing on your healing journey?

PHYSICAL:
What can you do to bring more happiness, peace, serenity, positive thoughts, and gratitude into your life? Remember, every day won't be sunshine and rainbows, but you can certainly bring more **joy** into your space by being intentional.

MENTAL:
How has your perception of trauma changed? How has it helped you understand experiences from your personal, family member's, or friend's life?

PAIN TO POWER PLAN

Transformation starts with you!

- Emotional
- Physical
- Mental

ACKNOWLEDGMENTS

I would like to thank my family, friends, and supporters for your motivation, trust, and believing in me on this journey of creating my first masterpiece.

I'd like to acknowledge those who have given this book, and the stories within it, legs strong enough to move forward:

April B.	Rose S.	Michelle L.
Kim A.	April W.	

I would like to express my sincere gratitude for the overwhelming outpour of support from the individuals who made this possible. You believed in me and my passion to serve people which brought my vision to reality. Thank you!

Adonis Randolph	Angelia Peete
Adyna Lungu	Anitra Appleby
Aisha Sidee	Anne Hoag
AJ Vann	Anthony D'Ambrosio
Alexis Truitt	Antoine Brumble
Altamese L. Burbage	Antoine Jackson

April Barrett
April N. Warren
Arnisha Hazelock
Arnita Gibson
Arthur Keene
Artish Fountain
Beatrice Adera
Belisha Bessick
Bernard Addogoh
Betty Manu
Bonnie Carr
Brigitte Debbie Mboumba
Bruce Ricketts
Carla Stanley
Carla Larrieu
Carnissa Pirtle
Carole Vincent
Carolyn Williams
Cassandra Payne
Chandra Phillips
Christina Mifflin
Clarissa Dennard
Cornell Stanley
Courtney Bateman
Curtis Dennard
Cynthia Goslee
Darrell Tingle
Deaira Tucker
Deborah Polk Peacock
Debra Fletcher
Denicia Youmens
Deidra Andrews

Derrick Anderson
Diane Winder
Donna Lewis
Erica Berry
Erica Smith
Eric Koester
Felicia Aline
Felicia Jackson
Fran Purnell
Garry Harris
Heather Phillips
Helena L. Hearn
Holly Applewhite
James Fletcher
James Brumble
Jamasine Matthews
Janika Duncan
Jason Gathright
Jean Banks-Miller
Jennifer Buckalew
Jill Rodelli
Joscelyn "JoJo" Varlack Hick's
Kahara Smith
Kathleen Raiford
Katrina Brumble
Kedra Box
Keila President
Kenneth M. Stronski
Kevin Jefferson
Kelley Conaway
Kelly Anderson
Keysha Robinson

Kiamishia Briggs
Kim Allison
Kimberly George
Kimberly Purnell
Kimolyn Barham
Kristin Wingate
Larnelle Robinson
Lilian Adera
Lisa R. Walker
Lois Brown
LuAnn Holden
Lyn Walters
Marcary Hopkins
MaryAnn Robinson-Gedeon
Marjorie Stewart
Marlene Mann
Marquetta Preston
Maurice Ojwang
Melissa James
Melissa King
Melvona Holley
Michele Brumble
Michelle Walker
Monica Long
Monica L. Speight
Monikia Cuffee
Monique Cornish
Niki Tate-Royal
Nikko Lee-Cannon
Octavia Cannon
Ralph Anderson
Rhondalin Cannon-Tingle
Rob Simek
Ronniece Williams
Rosa Jackson
Sabrina L. Horsey
Satish Shenoy
Scott Martin
Scott Navin
Sharon Flemz
Sharon McPhatter
Shawna Ward
Shawnta Corsey
Shysel Granados
Sonice Lee
Sonya Williams
Talmadge Reeves
Tamara Houston
Tanecha Fountain
Tanika Isler
Tanya Goodson
Taryn Flood
Teranissa Saunders
Teri Waters
Therman Winder
Tina Randolph
Tracey Phillips
Tricia Wingate
Trudy Waller
Vanessa Patel
Veronica H. Webb
Viola V. Banks
Wendy Willey

I would like to give a special shoutout to my mother, whom I often call "Momma Bear" because she is protective of her cubs; however, she has a heart of gold that is unmatched. I can't thank you enough for all the late nights just sitting with me in our "magic" room while I created content. What was special about those late-night moments were, in most cases, you would fall asleep on me, but it was just your presence in the room that kept me pushing. We can't forget about all the water, coffee, and snack runs to my bedroom and you never once complained. I could go on and on, but I will end here with a thank you for being my sounding board. When the tough got going, you pushed me through with your kind words and a gentle reminder I could do it. Here we are; cheers to you for being the real MVP of two amazing children.

I would like to extend my appreciation to two beautiful butterflies, Debra Fletcher and Joscelyn "JoJo" Varlack Hicks. Without you two paying it forward, I would've never been on this amazing journey. Thank you!

Lastly, but certainly not least, I would like to extend my heartfelt thank you to my tribe of friends who were my source of inspiration and motivation from day one.

A.J. Vann
Arnita Gibson
Antoine Brumble
B.D. Carter
Betty Manu
Ethel Williams
Kathleen Raiford

Larnelle Robinson
Lilian Adera
Marlene Mann
Michele Brumble
Monikia Cuffee
Monique Cornish
Rhondalin Cannon

APPENDIX

PROLOGUE

Howard, Logan D. "I've quit five jobs. I've given a two weeks' notice each time. l was let go each time before the two weeks were up." Picture. IFunny. October 12, 2019. *https://ifunny.co/picture/logan-d-howard-cpa-2nd-candidate-for-the-us-house-xPbqZnR67.*

INTRODUCTION

Czeisler, Mark E, Rashon I. Lane, Emiko Petrosky, Joshua F. Wiley, Aleta Christensen, Rashid Njai, Matthew D. Weaver, Rebecca Robbins, Elise R. Facer-Childs, Laura K. Barger, Charles A. Czeisler, Mark E. Howard, Shantha M. W. Rajaratnam. "Mental Health, Substance Use, and Suicidal Ideation During the COVID-19 Pandemic — United States, June 24–30, 2020." CDC, August 14, 2020. *https://www.cdc.gov/mmwr/volumes/69/wr/mm6932a1.htm.*

Fox, Mindy. "What Are Trauma Triggers and How to Identify Yours." mftherapy (blog), February 16, 2019. *https://mftherapy.com/trauma/what-are-trauma-triggers/.*

Gillihan, Seth J. "The COVID-19 Crisis May Trigger Emotions from Past Trauma." WebMD (blog), April 7, 2020. *https://blogs.webmd.com/mental-health/20200407/the-covid19-crisis-may-trigger-emotions-from-past-trauma.*

Humble, Amy and Whitney Johnson. "To Take Care of Others, Start by Taking Care of Yourself." Harvard Business Review, April 28, 2020. *https://hbr.org/2020/04/to-take-care-of-others-start-by-taking-care-of-yourself.*

King, Alanis. "Experts lay out how chaos caused by pandemic-era panic buying could revolutionize our global supply chain." The Business Insider, April 14, 2021. *https://www.businessinsider.com/supply-chain-pandemic-panic-buying-demand-dhl-order-ly-alom-technologies-2021-3?op=1.*

Merriam-Webster. s.v. "Trauma." Updated October 12, 2021. *https://www.merriam-webster.com/dictionary/trauma.*

CHAPTER 1

Adkins, Amy. "Millennials: The Job-Hopping Generation." Workplace, May 12, 2016. *https://www.gallup.com/workplace/236474/millennials-job-hopping-generation.aspx.*

Akhtar, Allana. "Elon Musk Said a College Degree Isn't Required for a Job at Tesla—And Apple, Google, and Netflix Don't Require Employees to Have 4-Year Degrees." The Business

Insider, December 27, 2020. *https://www.businessinsider.com/top-companies-are-hiring-more-candidates-without-a-4-year-degree-2019-4.*

Economy, Peter. "17 Things Every Successful Leader Says Every day." INC, August 22,2014. *https://www.inc.com/authour/peter-economy.*

Floyd, Tyler. "Hard Work Pays Off." Medium: Performance Course (blog), May 16th, 2020. *https://medium.com/performance-course/hard- link work-pays-off-46b4d5fff51a.*

Gillihan, Seth J. "The COVID-19 Crisis May Trigger Emotions from Past Trauma." WEBMD (blog), April 7, 2020. *https://blogs.webmd.com/mental-health/20200407/the-covid19-crisis-may-trigger-emotions-from-past-trauma.*

Lattimer, Christina. "Five Characteristic of An Open-Minded Leader." People Development Magazine, October 3, 2018. *https://peopledevelopmentmagazine.com/author/christinapd/.*

Luthi, Ben. "Why Career Planning is Important and How to Do It?" Chime (blog), May 2, 2018. *https://www.chime.com/blog/why-career-planning-is-important-and-how-to-do-it/.*

Meah, Asad. "You Can Do Anything that you set your mind to." Mindset. Awaken The Greatness Within. November 23, 2016. *https://www.awakenthegreatnesswithin.com/you-can-achieve-anything-that-you-set-your-mind-to/.*

Merriam-Webster. ed. s.v. "app (_n._)." Springfield: G & C Miriam Co., 1982. *https://www.merriam-webster.com/dictionary/trauma*.

Pelta, Rachel. "Education vs Experience: What Do Employers Want More?" Flexjobs.com (blog), February 12, 2021. *https://www.flexjobs.com/blog/post/education-vs-experience/*.

Sanin, Kyla. "Which Is More Important in Choosing a Career-Salary or Self-Fulfillment?" The Washington Post, November 29, 1990. *https://www.washingtonpost.com/archive/local/1990/11/29/which-is-more-important-in-choosing-a-career-salary-or-self-fulfillment/3e249557-9d59-445d-b922-ab1b4c65735e/*.

Shaw, George Bernard. "Don't wait for the right opportunity: create it." Good Reads.com. Accessed October 20, 2021. *https://www.goodreads.com/quotes/9536617-don-t-wait-for-the-right-opportunity-create-*.

St. Francis of Assisi. "Start by doing what's necessary; then do what's possible; and suddenly you are doing the impossible." Brainy Quote. Accessed October 19, 2021. *https://www.brainyquote.com/quotes/francis_of_assisi_121023*.

Via Satellite Magazine. "Elon Musk, Founder & Chief Engineer, SpaceX—SATELLITE 2020 Opening Day Keynote." March 9, 2019. Video, 47:18. *https://www.youtube.com/watch?v=HPV8Xp-3pEpI&feature=emb_logologo*.

Zig Ziglar. "If you can dream it, then you can achieve it. You will get all you want in life if you help enough other people get what they want." AZ Quotes. Accessed October 10,2021. *https://www.azquotes.com/quote/325027*.

CHAPTER 2

ABOVE INSPIRATION. "God Has a Plan for You | Chadwick Boseman." October 1, 2020. Video, 2:25. *https://www.youtube.com/watch?v=DoA-a-g204g*.

Heathfield, Susan M. "10 Things You Should Never Do When Firing an Employee, You Can Make the Experience Less Traumatic for All Parties Involved." thebalancecareers. February 28, 2021. *https://www.thebalancecareers.com/top-10-don-ts-when-you-fire-an-employee-1918343*.

Mayo Clinic Staff. "Spinal Stenosis." Diseases and Conditions. October 24, 2020. *https://www.mayoclinic.org/diseases-conditions/spinal-stenosis/symptoms-causes/syc-20352961*.

O'Donnell, J. T. "10 Things HR Doesn't Want You to Know (but I'll Tell You)" INC., Oct 6, 2015. *https://www.inc.com/jt-odonnell/10-things-hr-doesn-t-want-you-to-know-but-i-ll-tell-you.html*.

Pelta, Rachel. "Education vs Experience: What Do Employers Want More?" Flexjobs.com (blog), February 12, 2021. *https://www.flexjobs.com/blog/post/education-vs-experience/*.

CHAPTER 3

Cherry, Kendra. "How Social Support Contributes to Psychological Health." Very Well Mind. April 14, 2020. https://www.verywellmind.com/social-support-for-psychological-health-4119970.

Haas, Susan Biali M.D. "Journaling About Trauma and Stress Can Heal Your Body." Psychology Today (blog), December 7, 2019. https://www.psychologytoday.com/us/blog/prescriptions-life/201912/journaling-about-trauma-and-stress-can-heal-your-body.

Meekhof, Kristin. "5 Ways to Recover from Betrayal, have you been betrayed by a friend, lover or colleague?" Psychology Today (blog), May 14, 2019. https://www.psychologytoday.com/us/blog/widows-guide-healing/201905/5-ways-recover-betrayal.

O'Donnell, J. T. "10 Things HR Doesn't Want You to Know (but I'll Tell You)" INC., Oct 6, 2015. https://www.inc.com/jt-odonnell/10-things-hr-doesn-t-want-you-to-know-but-i-ll-tell-you.html.

Segal, Jeanne, Lawrence Robinson, Melinda Smith. "Emotional and Psychological Trauma." HelpGuide. February 2020. https://www.helpguide.org/articles/ptsd-trauma/coping-with-emotional-and-psychological-trauma.htm.

Waite, Jen. A Beautiful, Terrible Thing: A Memoir of Marriage and Betrayal. New York: Plume Books, 2017.

CHAPTER 4

Chater, Angel, Julia Fruer, Neil Howlett, William Gillian Shorter, and Jane Zakrzewski. "Can Physical Activity Support Grief

Outcomes in Individuals Who Have Been Bereaved: A Systematic Review?" Sports Medicine. Accessed October 15, 2021. https://www.researchgate.net/publication/350748350_Can_Physical_Activity_Support_Grief_Outcomes_in_Individuals_Who_Have_Been_Bereaved_A_Systematic_Review.

Hawkins, John Jr. "STAGES OF GRIEF: THE 7 STAGES OF GRIEF EXPLAINED." Gateway Counseling Center (blog), March 14, 2017. https://gatewaycounseling.com/7-stages-of-grief-explained/.

Maya Angelou. "I can be changed by what happens to me. But I refuse to be reduced by it." Good Reads.com. Accessed October 21. https://www.goodreads.com/author/quotes/3503.Maya_Angelou.

Mayo Clinic. "What is Grief?" Support & bereavement group. October 19, 2016. https://www.mayoclinic.org/patient-visitor-guide/support-groups/what-is-grief.

Richards, Sarah Elizabeth. "Sweating Out the Sadness: Can Exercise Help You Grieve?" HuffPost, updated June 10, 2014. https://www.huffpost.com/entry/exercise-grief-sadness_n_5474993.

Rose, Hannah. "When It's Okay to Not Be Okay." Psychology Today (blog), July 5, 2019. https://www.psychologytoday.com/us/blog/working-through-shame/201907/when-its-okay-not-be-okay.

Wolfet, Alan D. PhD. "Embracing the Sadness of Grief." Center for Loss. February 4, 2016. https://www.centerforloss.com/2016/02/embracing-the-sadness-of-grief/.

CHAPTER 5

Bay, Rachael A., Noah Rose, Rowan Barrett, Louis Bernatchez, Cameron K. Ghalambor, Jesse R. Lasky, Rachel B. Brem, Stephen R. Palumbi, and Peter Ralph. "Predicting Responses to Contemporary Environmental Change Using Evolutionary Response Architectures." American Naturalist 189, no. 5 (May 2017): 463–73. *https://doi.org/10.1086/691233*.

Elevated Faith (blog). "HOW TO TRUST GOD THROUGH THE STORM." January 17, 2018. *https://elevatedfaith.com/blogs/elevated-faith-blog/how-to-trust-god-through-the-storm?page=3*.

Henderson, Wendy. "10 Common Emotional Responses to a Cancer Diagnosis." BioNews Services, May 8, 2017. *https://breastcancer-news.com/2017/05/08/10-common-emotional-responses-cancer-diagnosis/*.

Logan Sport Memorial Hospital (blog). "Why Self-Breast Exams Are Important (And How to Do them)." Accessed September 25, 2021. *https://blog.logansportmemorial.org/why-self-breast-exams-are-important-and-how-to-do-them*.

Mayo Clinic Staff. "Support groups: Make connections, get help." Mayo Clinic. August 29, 2020. *https://www.mayoclinic.org/healthy-lifestyle/stress-management/in-depth/support-groups/art-20044655*.

Shaw, Gina. "Breast Cancer Survivors: Life After the Treatments End." WebMD. Accessed September 25, 2021. *https://www.webmd.com/breast-cancer/features/life-after-breast-cancer-treatment*.

CHAPTER 6

Doyle, Alison. "Inspirational Quotes About Hard Work." the balance careers, updated March 7, 2020. *https://www.thebalancecareers.com/quotes-about-hard-work-2062837.*

Hall, Alena. "8 Celebrities Who Transformed Tragedy into Something Positive." HuffPost, December 6, 2017. *https://www.huffpost.com/entry/celebrities-overcoming-loss_n_5669363.*

Klinge, Dawn. "How to Quiet Your Mind So You Can Hear from God." Dawn Klinge (blog), January 10, 2018. *https://www.dawnklinge.com/abovethewaves/how-to-quiet-your-mind-so-you-can-hear-from-god.*

Mason, Tiffany. "Four Proven Ways to Overcome Adversity." Psych Central (blog), March 30, 2014. *https://psychcentral.com/blog/4-proven-ways-to-overcome-adversity#2.*

Merriam-Webster. s.v. "Adversity." Accessed September 26, 2021. *https://www.merriam-webster.com/dictionary/adversity.*

Psychology Today Staff. "Post-Traumatic Growth." Psychology Today. Accessed October 15, 2021. *https://www.psychologytoday.com/us/basics/post-traumatic-growth.*

Saunders, Kevin. "Overcome Adversity and Conquer Your Goals." Labrada (blog), accessed September 27, 2021. *https://www.labrada.com/blog/motivational/tips-to-overcoming-any-adversity-achieving-your-dream-lean-body-in-the-new-year/.*

TED. "Thriving in the Face of Adversity" | Stephanie Buxhoeveden." April 3, 2015. Video, 17:43. *https://www.youtube.com/watch?v=zuLOT6GsAxw.*

Thompson, Zach. "Simone Biles: Overcoming Adversity to Become the GOAT." DraftKings Nation, August 30, 2021. *https://dknation.draftkings.com/playbook/22645773/simone-biles-overcoming-adversity-to-become-the-goat-draftkings-marketplace-nft-olympics-gymnastics.*

CHAPTER 7

Brown, Dawn. "How To Know If You Are Depressed: 11 Signs to Notice and When to Get Help." Advice. Better Help. August 28, 2020. *https://www.betterhelp.com/advice/depression/how-to-know-if-you-are-depressed-11-signs-to-notice-and-when-to-get-help/.*

Center for Disease Control and Prevention. "Suicide rising across the U.S. More than a mental health concern." Accessed September 30, 2021. *https://www.cdc.gov/vitalsigns/suicide/index.html.*

Federal Communications Commission. Fact Sheet: 988 and Suicide Prevention Hotline. Atlanta: FCC.gov, 2021. *https://www.fcc.gov/sites/default/files/988-fact-sheet.pdf.*

Firestone, Lisa. "It's Not Your Fault: Overcoming Trauma: The importance of accepting that we are not to blame for our trauma." Psychology Today (blog), May 21, 2018. *https://www.psychologytoday.com/us/blog/compassion-matters/201805/it-s-not-your-fault-overcoming-trauma.*

Harvard Women's Health Watch. "Suicide Survivors Face grief, questions, challenges." Harvard Health Blog, June 15, 2020. *https://www.health.harvard.edu/blog/suicide-survivors-face-grief-questions-challenges-201408127342.*

Harvard Health Publishing (blog). "Left behind after suicide." Mind and Mood. May 29, 2019. *https://www.health.harvard.edu/mind-and-mood/left-behind-after-suicide.*

Mental Health Daily. "10 Powerful Suicide Prevention Quotes & Sayings." Accessed October 4, 2021. *https://mentalhealthdaily.com/2014/09/24/10-powerful-suicide-prevention-quotes-sayings/.*

National Suicide Prevention Lifeline. "Home Page." Accessed October 4, 2021. *https://suicidepreventionlifeline.org/.*

Skerrett, Patrick J. "Suicide often not preceded by warnings." Harvard Health Blog, September 24, 2012. *https://www.health.harvard.edu/blog/suicide-often-not-preceded-by-warnings-201209245331.*

CHAPTER 8

Butler, Kristen. "10 Ways to Get Negative Thoughts Out (And Let Positive Thoughts In)." Medium (blog), June 7, 2020. *https://medium.com/@Kristen_Butler/10-ways-to-get-negative-thoughts-out-and-let-positive-thoughts-in-3a77f7542664.*

Canfield, Jack. "5 Tips to Stop Negative Self-Talk Once & For All." Life and Spirituality. Jack Canfield, Maximizing Your Potential (blog), accessed October 1, 2021. *https://www.jackcanfield.com/blog/negative-self-talk/.*

Economy, Peter. "17 Powerfully Inspiring Quotes to Overcome Any Insecurity." INC, April 7, 2019. *https://www.inc.com/peter-economy/17-powerfully-inspiring-quotes-to-overcome-any-insecurity.html.*

Jamieson, Alexandra. "How Negative Self-Talk Is Killing Your Health and Weight-Loss Goals." US News (blog), June 9, 2015. *https://health.usnews.com/health-news/blogs/eat-run/2015/06/09/how-negative-self-talk-is-killing-your-health-and-weight-loss-goals.*

Mayo Clinic Staff. "Stress management, Positive thinking: Stop negative self-talk to reduce stress." Accessed October 1, 2021. *https://www.mayoclinic.org/healthy-lifestyle/stress-management/in-depth/positive-thinking/art-20043950.*

Moore, Catherine. "Positive Daily Affirmations: Is There Science Behind It?" Positive Psychology (blog), March 16, 2021. *https://positivepsychology.com/daily-affirmations/.*

Morin, Amy. "5 Ways to Turn Your Negative Self-Talk into a More Productive Inner Dialogue: Negative self-talk will prevent you from living a positive life. Here's how to create a more powerful inner dialogue." Startup Life. INC., April 3, 2018. *https://www.inc.com/amy-morin/how-to-deal-with-your-negative-self-talk-so-you-can-stop-beating-yourself-up-dragging-yourself-down.html.*

O'Brien, Pamela. "Your Negative Self-Talk Could Be Harming Your Health — Here's How to Stop." Shape, June 22, 2021. *https://www.shape.com/lifestyle/mind-and-body/negative-self-talk-health-impact.*

Power of Positivity. "10 Ways to Get Negative Thoughts Out (And Let Positive Thoughts In)." Updated December 21, 2019. Accessed October 1, 2021. https://www.powerofpositivity.com/negative-thoughts-out-positive-thoughts-in/.

Robinson, Lawrence, Jeanne Segal, and Melinda Smith. "The Mental Health Benefits of Exercise." Exercise & Fitness. Helpguide. Last Updated August 2021. Accessed October 1, 2021. https://www.helpguide.org/articles/healthy-living/the-mental-health-benefits-of-exercise.htm.

CHAPTER 9

Denny, Katherine G. and Hans Steiner. "External and Internal Factors Influencing Happiness in Elite Collegiate Athletes." National Library of Medicine, 40(1):55-72. doi: 10.1007/s10578-008-0111-z. https://pubmed.ncbi.nlm.nih.gov/18626767/.

Dohling, Thomas. "Meaningful Quotes, Daily Dose of meaningful. motivational, inspirational, positive quotes from various sources." November 23, 2017. https://meaningfulquotesweb.wordpress.com/2017/11/23/ive-learned/.

Fox, Mindy. "What Are Trauma Triggers and How to Identify Yours." mftherapy (blog), February 16, 2019. https://mftherapy.com/trauma/what-are-trauma-triggers/.

Gandhi, Bela. "8 Ways to Crush 2020." Harvey's Hundred. Steve Harvey.com. Accessed October 1, 2021. https://steveharvey.com/8-ways-to-crush-2020/.

Greater Good Magazine. "Mindfulness Defined." Accessed October 15, 2021. *https://greatergood.berkeley.edu/topic/mindfulness/definition.*

Hale, Mandy. "Happiness is an inside job. Don't assign anyone else that much power over your life." Thrive Global. Accessed October 19, 2021. *https://thriveglobal.com/stories/happiness-inside-job-advice-life/.*

Hugo. "How Happiness Is an Inside Job (Researched Tips and Examples)." Tracking Happiness, published January 10, 2020. Updated July 19, 2021. *https://www.trackinghappiness.com/happiness-is-an-inside-job/.*

Jack Canfield. "How To Deal with Negative Self-Talk." April 26, 2018. Video, 8:08. *https://www.youtube.com/watch?v=h5iZ6ntDlHk.*

Lum, Kathleen. "9 Ways to Truly Find Happiness Within Yourself." LifeHack (blog), accessed September 24, 2021. *https://www.lifehack.org/463189/9-ways-to-truly-find-happiness-within-yourself.*

Maya Angelou. "I've learned that no matter what happens, or how bad it seems today, life does go on, and it will be better tomorrow." GoodReads.com May 29, 2021. *https://www.goodreads.com/quotes/5141700-i-ve-learned-that-no-matter-what-happens-or-how-bad.*

"Mindfulness Defined." Greater Good Magazine, October 14, 2021. *https://greatergood.berkeley.edu/topic/mindfulness.*

Moore, Catherine. "Positive Daily Affirmations: Is There Science Behind It?" Positive Psychology (blog), March 16, 2021. https://positivepsychology.com/daily-affirmations/.

Robertson, Catherine. "How Gratitude Can Change Your Life." Rick Hanson, PhD. Accessed September 25, 2021. https://www.rickhanson.net/how-gratitude-can-change-your-life/.

Science of Happiness Podcast. "Mindfulness Defined." Greater Good Magazine, October 14, 2021. https://greatergood.berkeley.edu/topic/mindfulness.

Sharpe, Rachel. "90+ Inspiring Dalai Lama Quotes to Change Your Outlook on Life." Declutter the Mind (blog), December 22, 2020. https://declutterthemind.com/blog/dalai-lama-quotes/.

Thornton, Andy. "The Importance of Kindness." Foothold (blog), September 25, 2021. https://www.myfoothold.org/blog/the-importance-of-kindness/.

Tzu, Lao. Tao Te Ching. Mineola: Ixia Press- Dover Publications, 2016.

CHAPTER 10

Breene, Sophia. "13 Mental Health Benefits of Exercise." HuffPost, updated December 6, 2017. https://www.huffpost.com/entry/mental-health-benefits-exercise_n_2956099.

CDC.gov. Coping with Stress After a Traumatic Event: Tip Sheet. Atlanta: CDC.gov, 2017. https://www.cdc.gov/violenceprevention/pdf/CopingwithStress.pdf.

Henderson, Abbi. "Positive Affirmations: How Do They Work, Are They Science-backed and 13 to Try." Women's Health, April 26, 2021. https://www.womenshealthmag.com/uk/health/mental-health/a36198569/positive-affirmations/.

John Hopkins Medicine. "Keep Your Brain Young with Music." Accessed September 27, 2021. https://www.hopkinsmedicine.org/health/wellness-and-prevention/keep-your-brain-young-with-music.

Lyiscott, Jamila. "3 Ways to Speak English." Filmed February 2014 in New York, NY. TED video, 4:29. https://www.ted.com/talks/jamila_lyiscott_3_ways_to_speak_english.

Maze, Victor. "5 Decluttering Experts Share the Tips and Inspiration You Need Right Now." Veranda Bloomingdale's. April 10, 2020. https://www.veranda.com/home-decorators/g32099980/decluttering-tips-resources/.

Reed, Katie. "34 Self-Care Quotes: A Little Nudge to Prioritize Yourself!" Goal Chaser (blog) accessed October 4, 2021. https://thegoalchaser.com/self-care-quotes/.

Shoaf, Noah. "Editorial: Limiting social media benefits health and happiness." The Leader Kealakai, January 30, 2020. https://kealakai.byuh.edu/editorial-limiting-social-media-benefits-health-and-happiness.

TED. "12 truths I learned from life and writing | Anne Lamott." July 13, 2017. Video, 15:54. https://www.youtube.com/watch?v=X-41iulkRqZU.

University of Notre Dame. "Taking Care of Yourself after a Traumatic Event." University Counseling Center. Accessed September 27, 2021. *https://ucc.nd.edu/self-help/disaster-trauma/taking-care-of-yourself/*.

CONCLUSION

Bishop, T.D. Jakes. "Trauma, Triggers, and Triumph| Bishop T.D. Jakes." January 17, 2021. Video, 1:21:46. *https://www.youtube.com/watch?v=HzujSUnYUyQ*.

www.ingramcontent.com/pod-product-compliance
Lightning Source LLC
LaVergne TN
LVHW011827060526
838200LV00053B/3926